METEORITES: OUTER SPACE ART 1

RICK CONNER

Published in 2019

Copyright © Rick Conner 2019

All rights reserved.

The information contained in this book is both true and complete to the best of the author's knowledge. All photos with accompanying information come from known examples found.

No part of this book may be used or reproduced without written permission from the author.

Visit Amazon.com to see additional book titles by this author.

On the front cover: Chug-Chug 009

Cover design, imaging and technical assistance: Connie Conner

Dedicated to all ages of art lovers and collectors of ancient meteorites or outer space.

INTRODUCTION

Meteorites: Outer Space Art 1 showcases a selection of thinly cut and polished meteorite slices specifically chosen for their unique artistic patterns. The art work created inside of some meteorites after tumbling through space is more beautiful than the dark and dull exterior now sculpted by the heat into various shapes. Color close-up photographs of selected polished meteorite sections highlight each of their unique artistic qualities. Displayed are a variety of natural color patterns, the glow of gemlike translucent olivines and the intricacy of Widmanstatten patterns.

What mankind calls "shooting stars" or "falling stars" are scientifically called meteors, and after impact, those pieces are called meteorites. Most meteors hit our atmosphere and burn up entirely and that is especially true for the stone ones because they are softer than the iron ones.

A few meteorites are found to originate from the Moon and Mars when chunks of those planets are knocked into orbit after asteroid strikes. But, after comparing meteorite compositions, scientists can verify most meteorites actually come from asteroids.

So quite literally meteorites are rocks that drop out of the sky. Most meteorites are the oldest material found on our planet and date from the earliest time of the solar system. When found they are always named for the places they were found, usually a town or geographic feature, and when several meteorites are found in one place the name could be followed by either a number or letter. A meteorite is then classified into one of three broad categories. The largest group at 86% and most common are stony meteorites called chondrites that contain small grains of nickel-iron evenly distributed throughout, and many have small balls of stony material inside called chondrules. Another 8% of meteorites found are termed achondrites which means they do not contain chondrules and are very similar to terrestrial igneous rocks. The third largest group at 5%, or only one in ten meteorites that fall on Earth, are the iron meteorites composed of iron-nickel alloys with a dense, silvery looking interior without crystals or holes. Finally, the rarest at 1% are the stony-iron meteorites composed of characteristics of both the chondrite and iron types being comprised roughly of half metal and half crystals with some mineral portions of dark silicate minerals or yellowish green, yellowish brown or orange olivine crystals. One type classified as pallasite possibly originated in the boundary zone above the core regions where iron meteorites originate. Pallasites are asteroids that have undergone a thermal differentiation process. Another major type of stony-iron meteorites is a mesosiderite consisting of about equal parts metallic nickel-iron and silicate.

March 2015 was the first time NASA scientists reported complex organic compounds were found in DNA and RNA including uracil, cytosine and thymine, having been formed in a laboratory under precise outer space conditions including using starting chemicals such as pyrimidine found in meteorites. According to scientists, pyrimidine is the most carbon-rich chemical found in the Universe and probably formed inside either red giants or interstellar dust and gas clouds.

Then in January 2018, after researching 4.5 billion-year-old meteorites found on Earth, scientists discovered that they contained not only liquid water but also prebiotic complex organic substances which very well could be ingredients for life.

TABLE OF CONTENTS

ABA PANU: Found April 19, 2018 around the village of Aba Panu in the State of Oyo, Nigeria, Africa 5

ADMIRE: Found 1881 in Lyon County, Kansas, USA 10

ALETAI: Found 1898 and named after Aletai County in the northern part of Xinjiang Uyghur Autonomous Region, China 11

AYAGOZ: Found 2000 in the prairie 12 km south of Ayagoz, Kazakhstan 12

BRAHIN: Found 1807 by farmers of Kaporenki, a village in the district of Bragin, Gomel Region, Belarus 13

BRENHAM: Found 1885 near the town of Haviland in Kiowa County, Kansas, United States where it fell to earth some 1000-2000 years ago 15

CALAMA 005: Found March 25, 2017 in the Province of Antofagasta, Chile 17

CALAMA 006: Found March 15, 2017 in the Province of Antofagasta, Chile 19

CALAMA 020: Found October 15, 2017 in the Province of Antofagasta, Chile 21

CALAMA 022: Found October 15, 2017 near the village of Chiu Chiu in the Province of Antofagasta, Chile 23

CAMPO DEL CIELO: Found 1576 in Argentina 25

CHUG-CHUG 004: Found March 29, 2018 in the Province of Antofagasta, Chile 26

CHUG-CHUG 009: Found October 13, 2018 in the Province of Antofagasta, Chile 28

CHUG-CHUG 011: Found October 13, 2018 in the Province of Antofagasta, Chile 30

CLARENDON: Found April 6, 2015 near Clarendon, Texas, USA 32

CONCEPTION JUNCTION: Found 2006 protruding from a hillside near Conception Junction, Missouri, USA 36

ESQUEL: Found 1951 near the Patagonian town of Esquel in the northwest part of the Province of Chubut, Argentina 37

FUKANG: Found 2000 in the mountains near Fukang, Xinjiang Province, China 39

ABA PANU

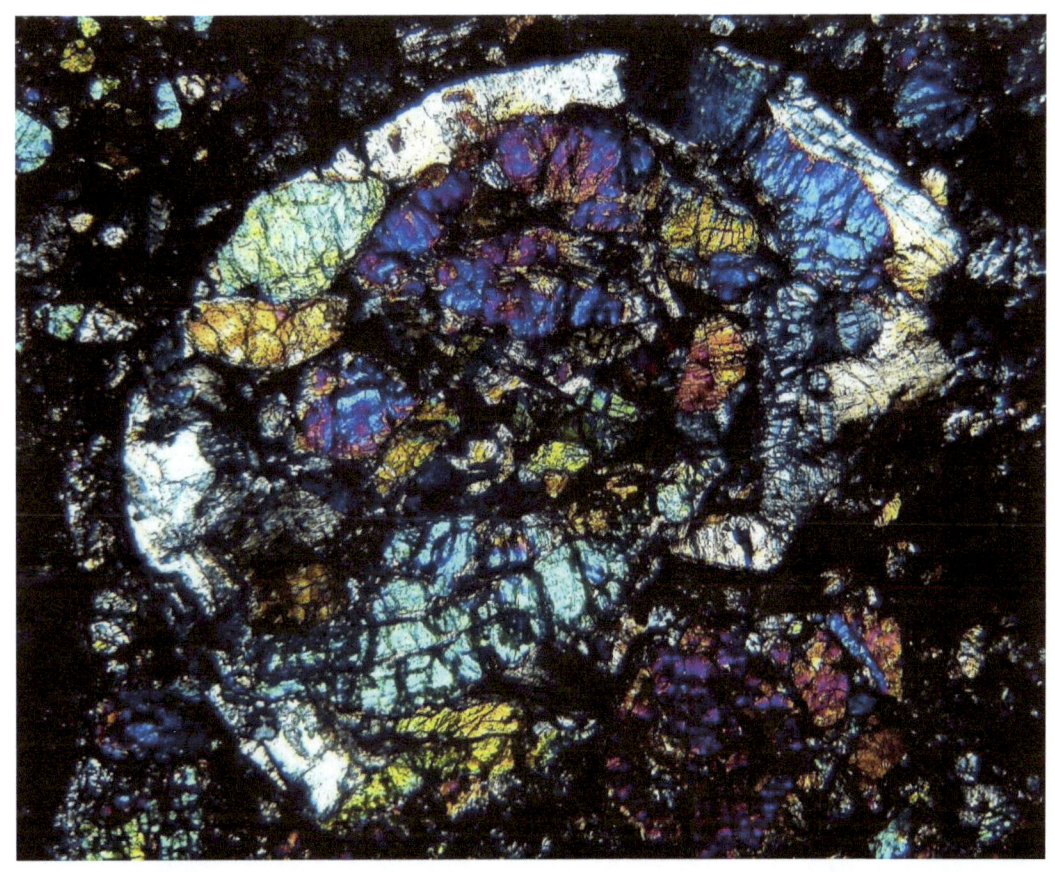

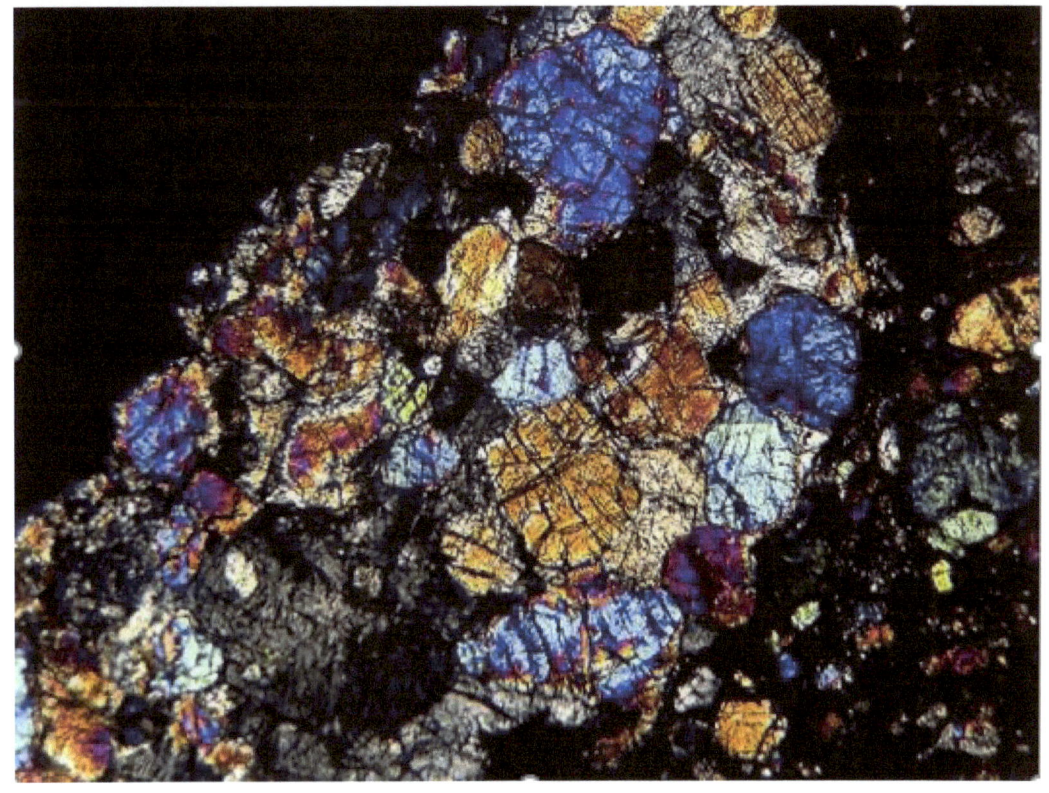

ABA PANU

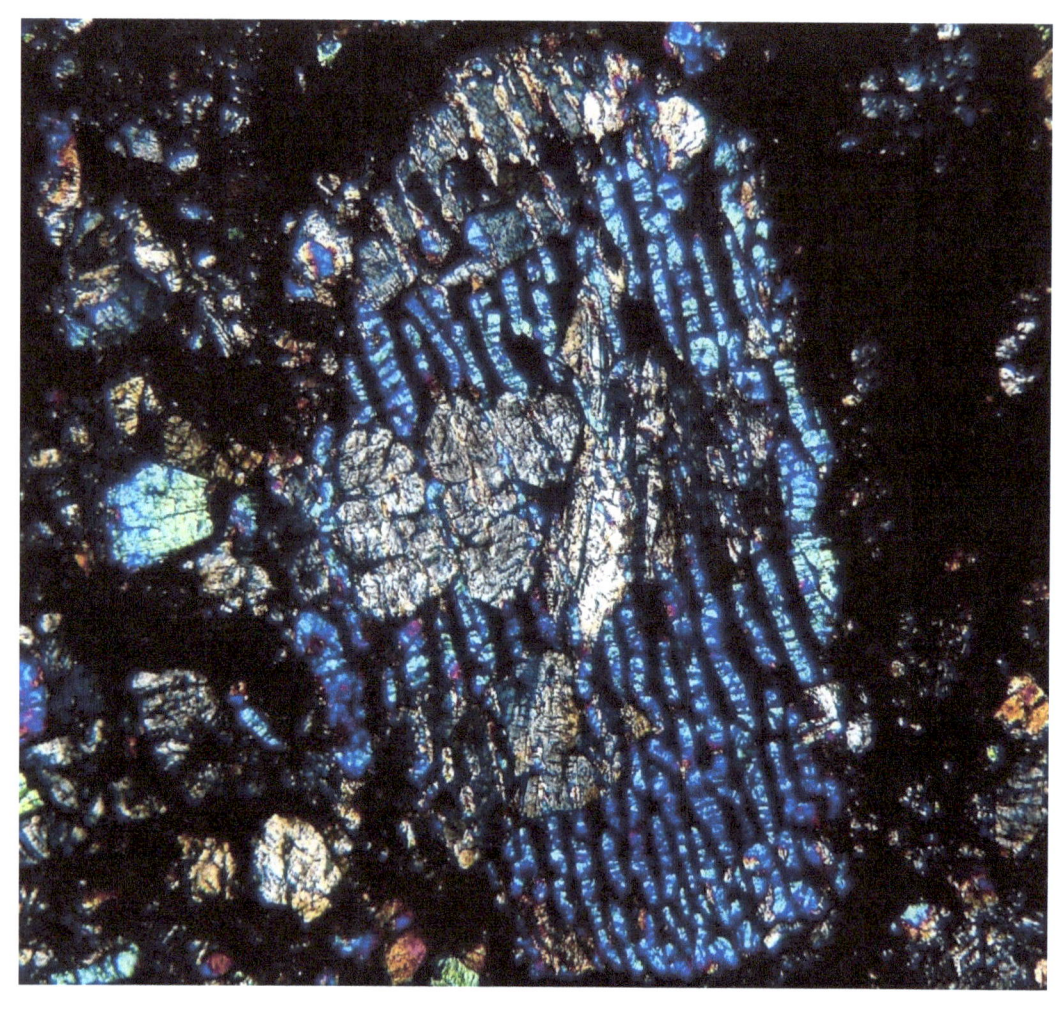

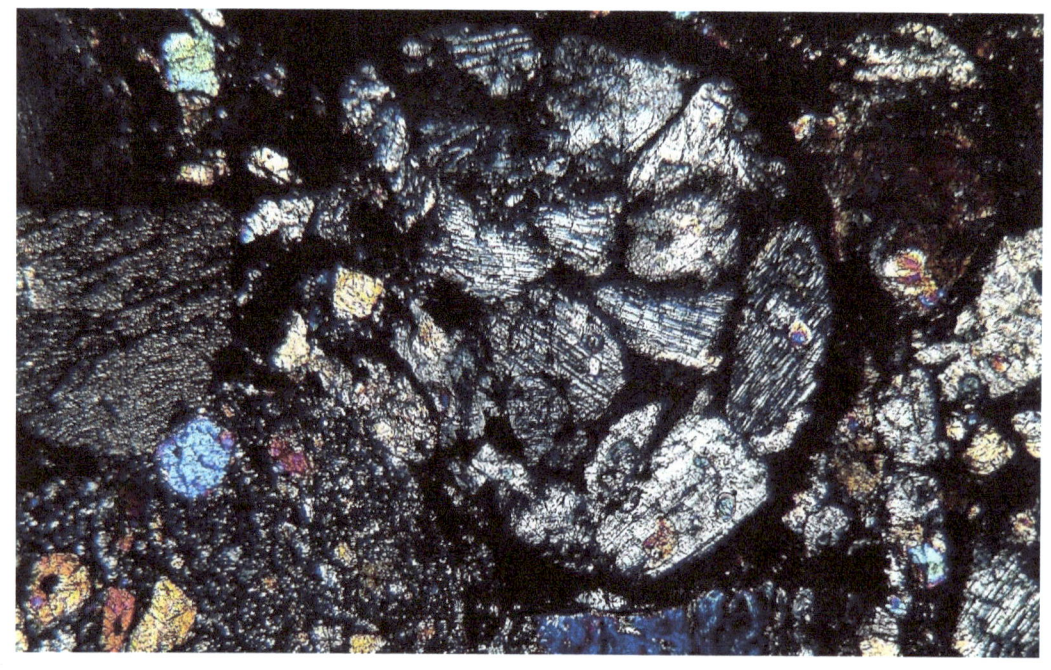

ABA PANU

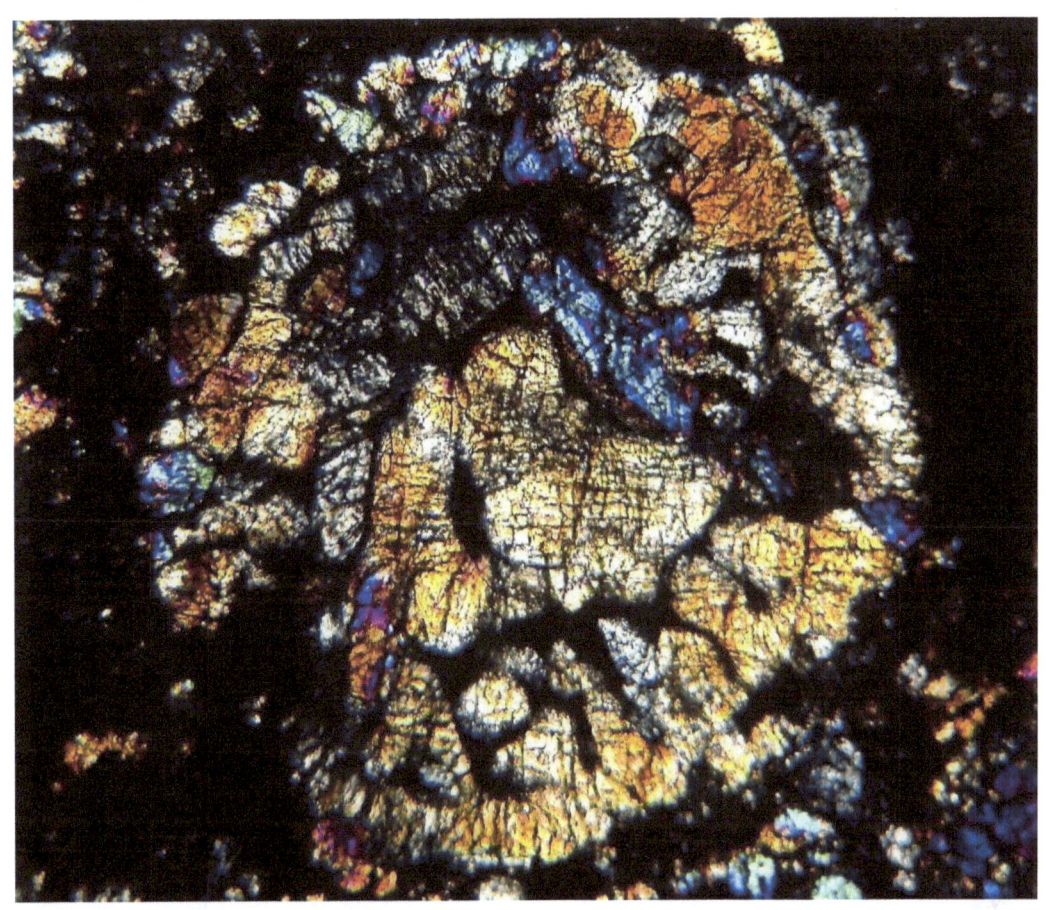

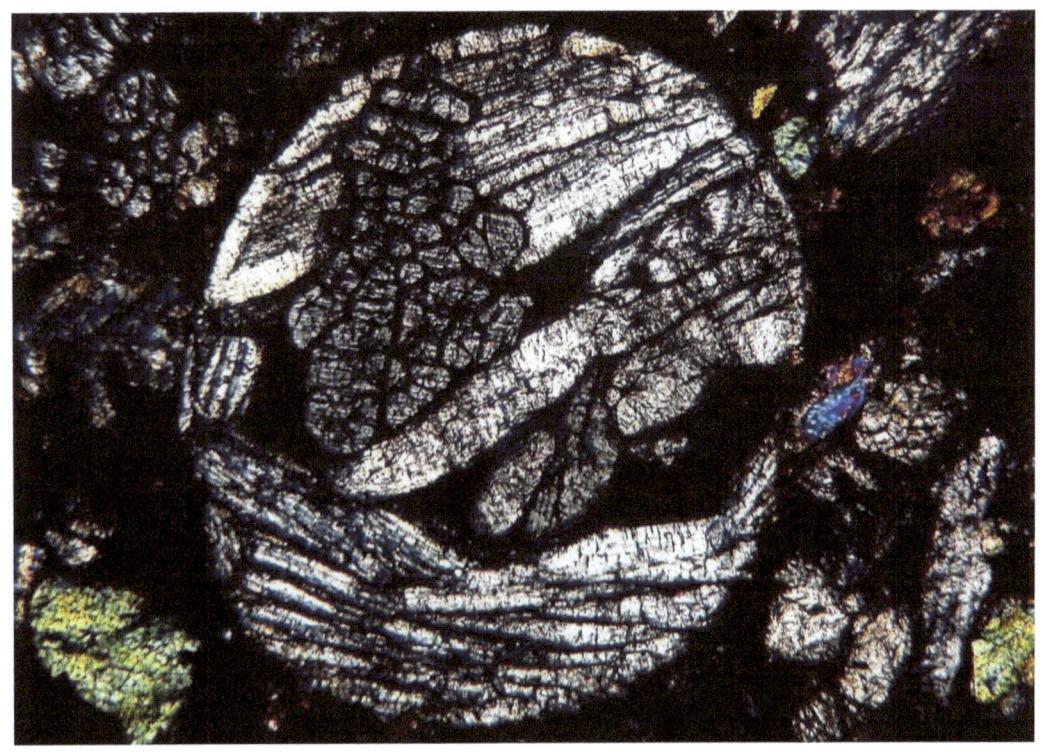

ABA PANU

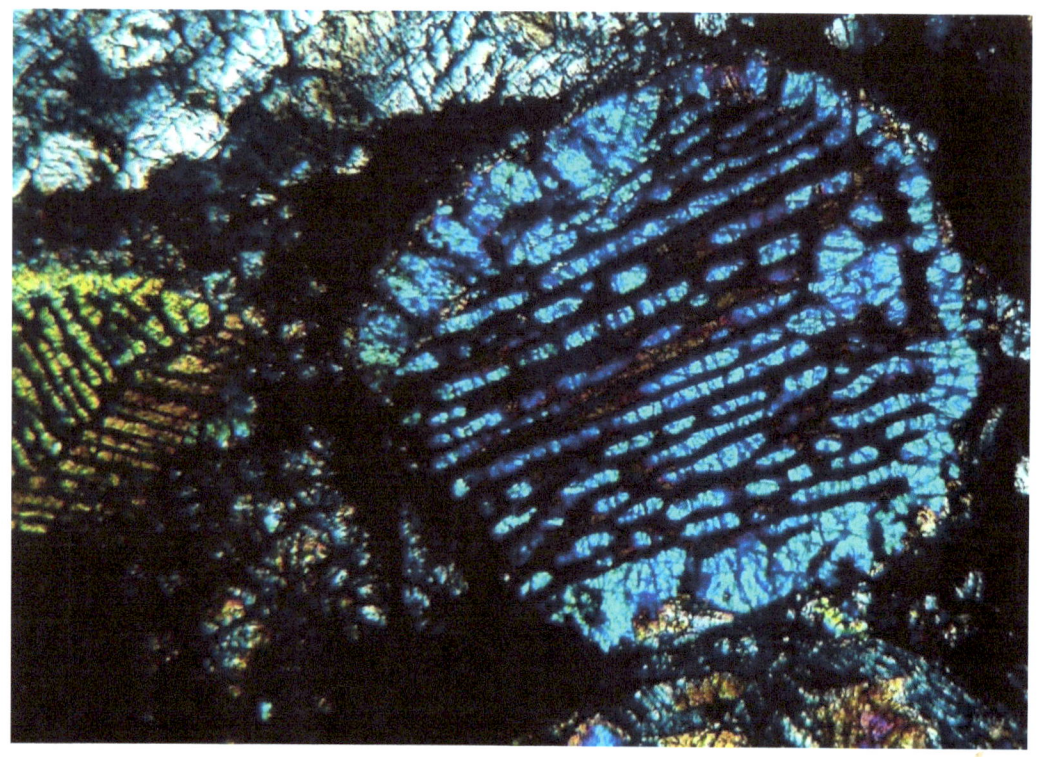

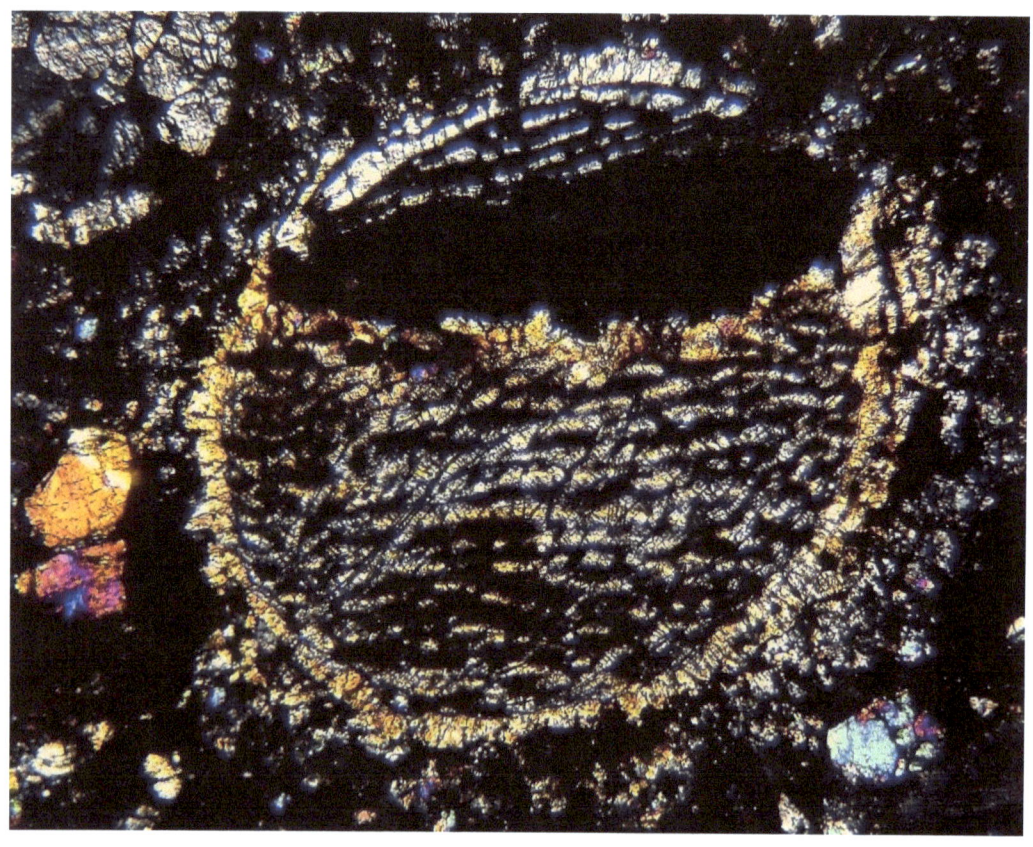

ABA PANU

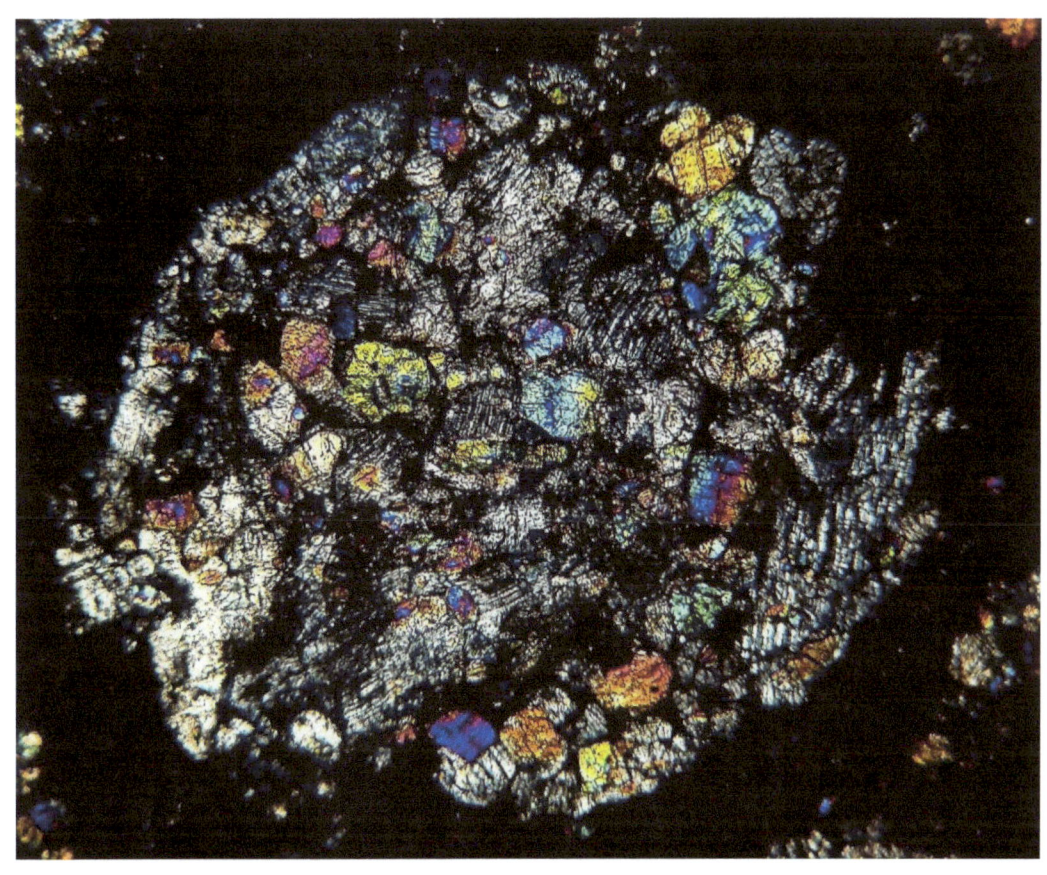

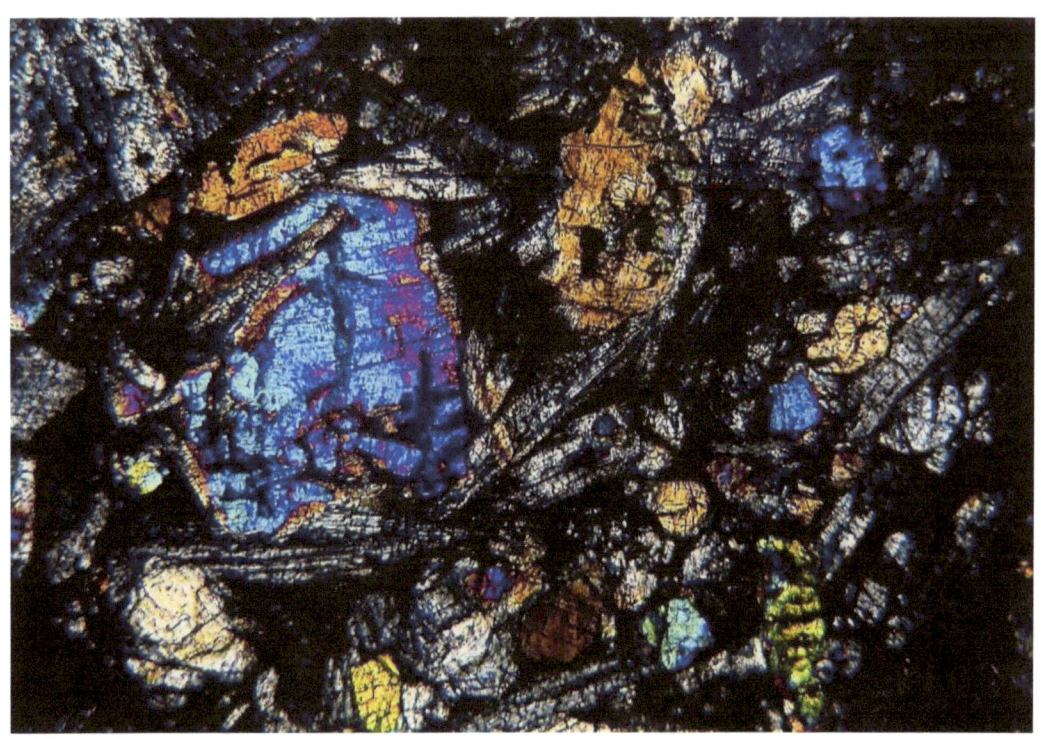

ADMIRE

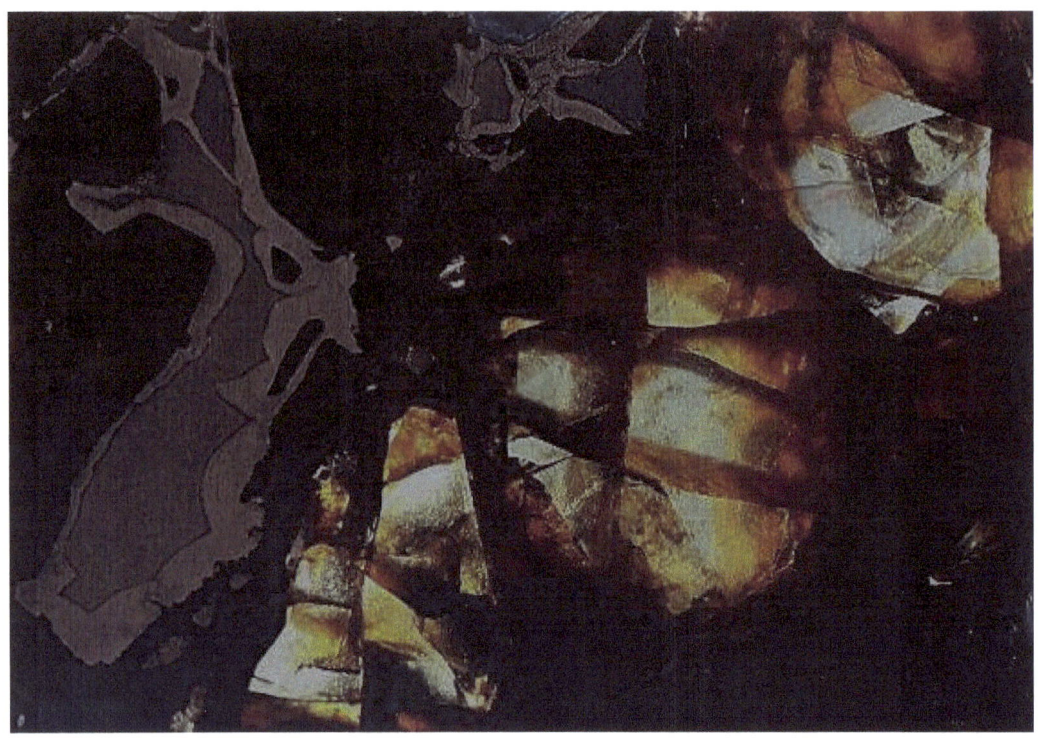

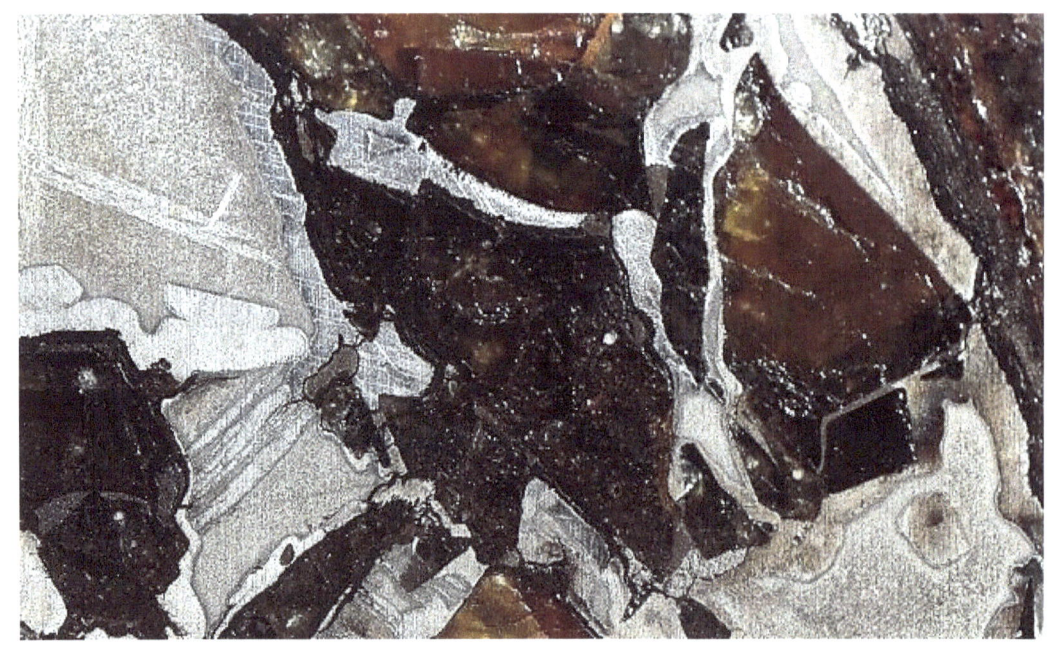

ALETAI

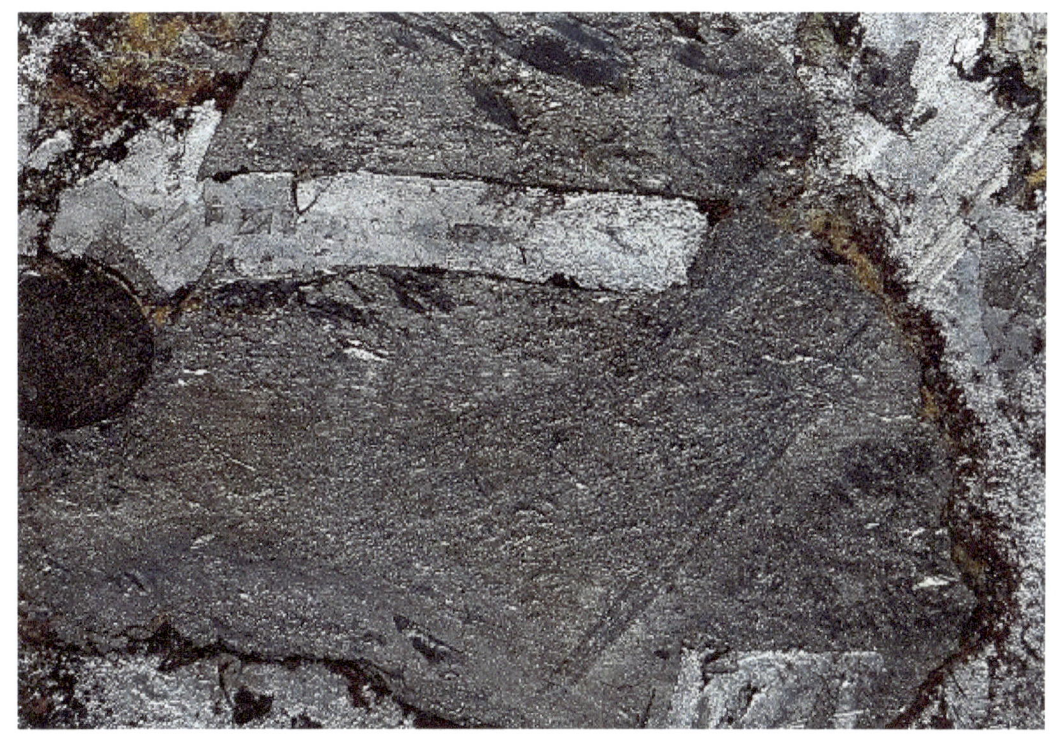

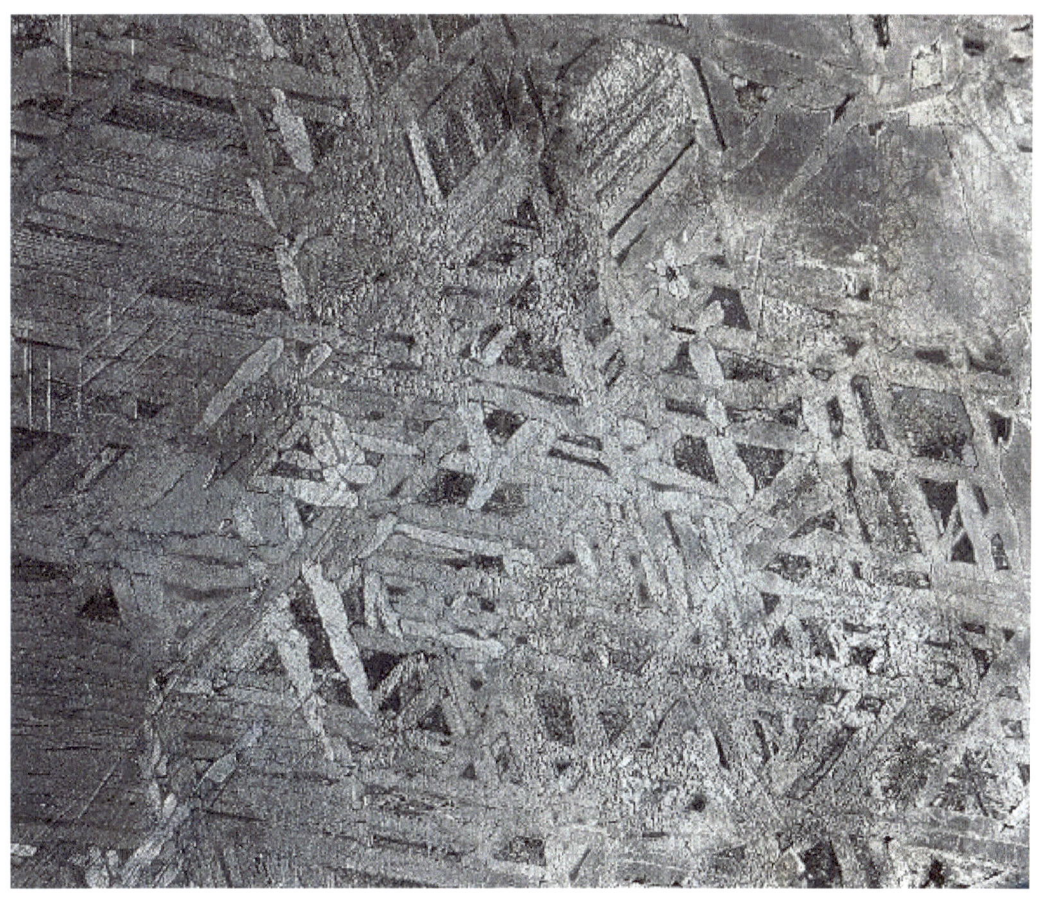

AYAGOZ

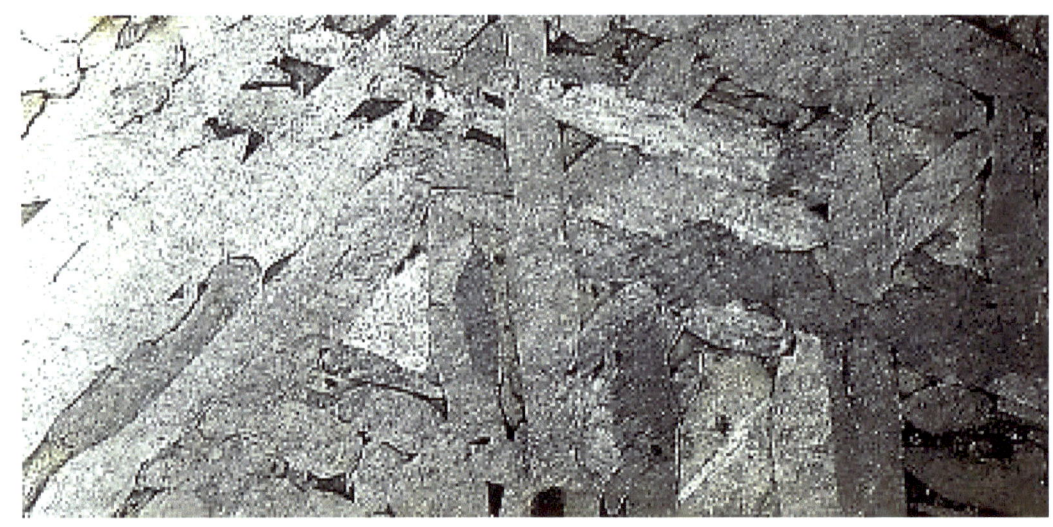

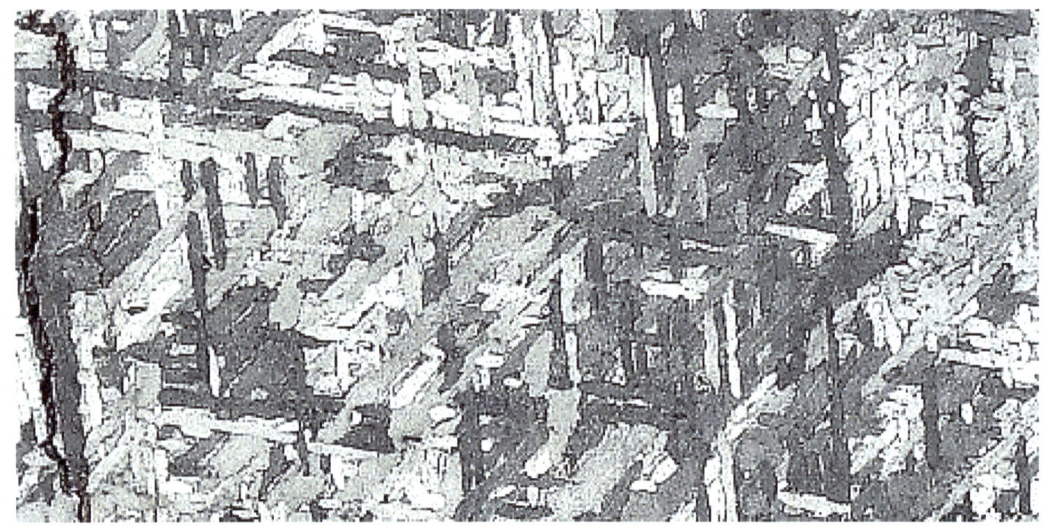

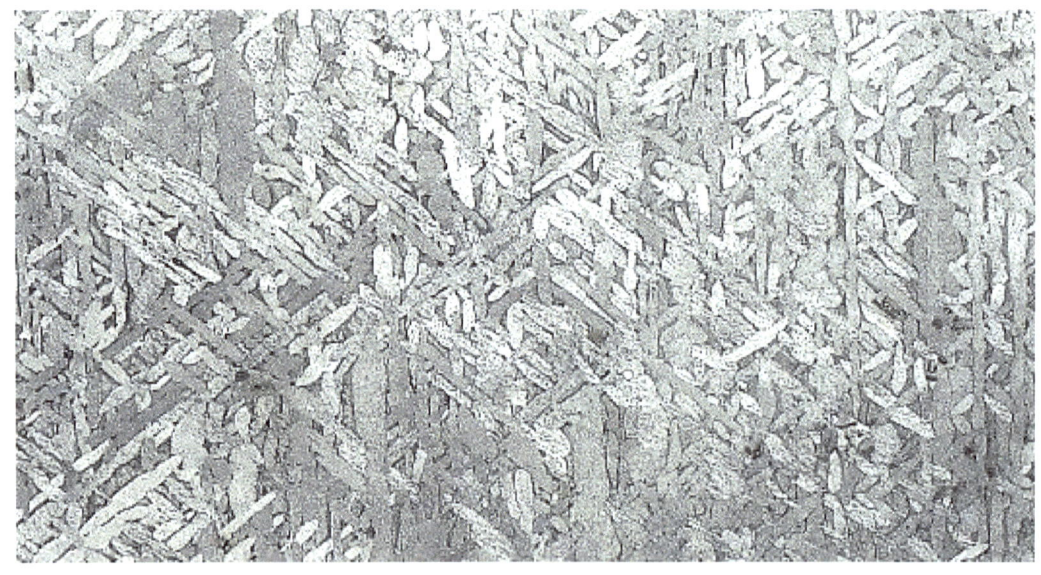

BRAHIN

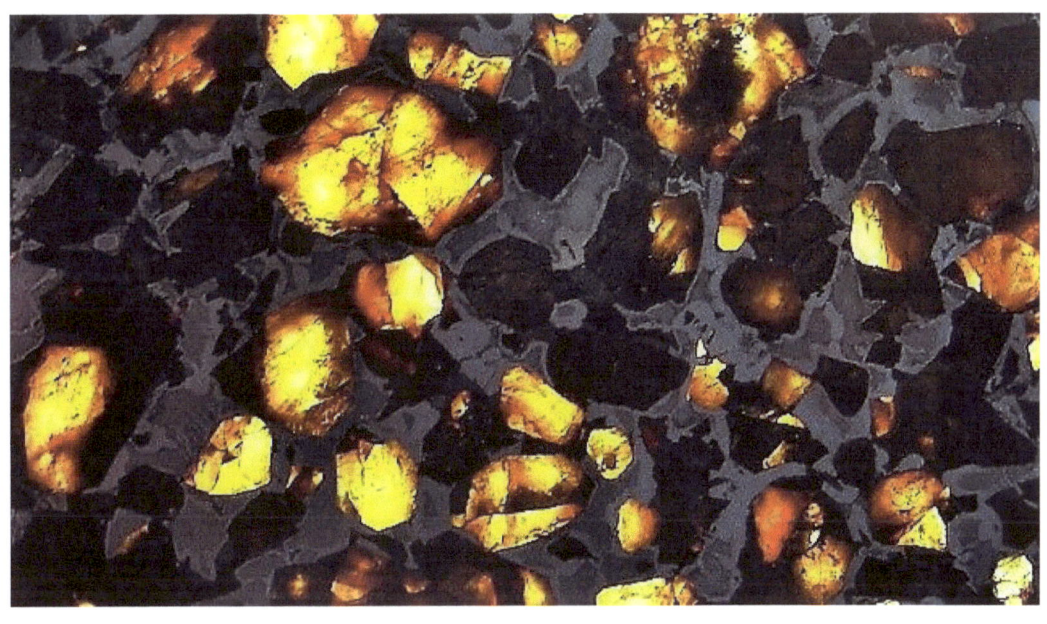

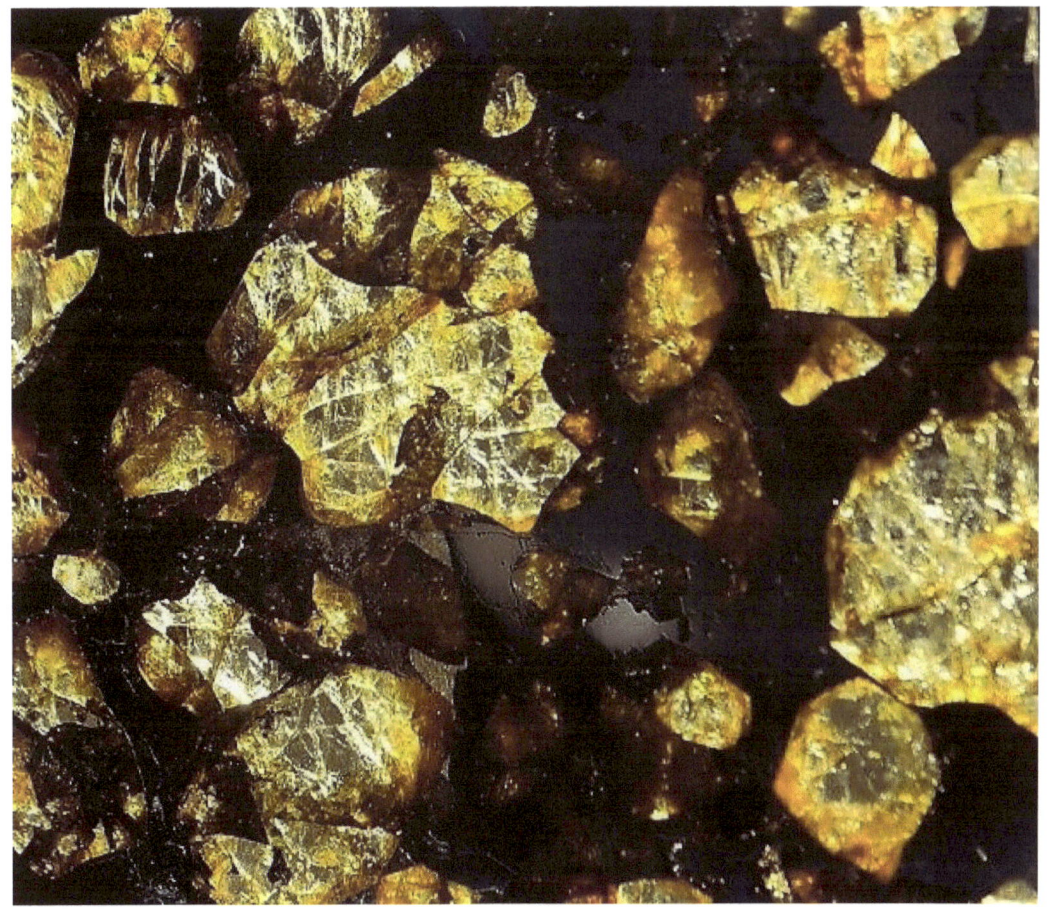

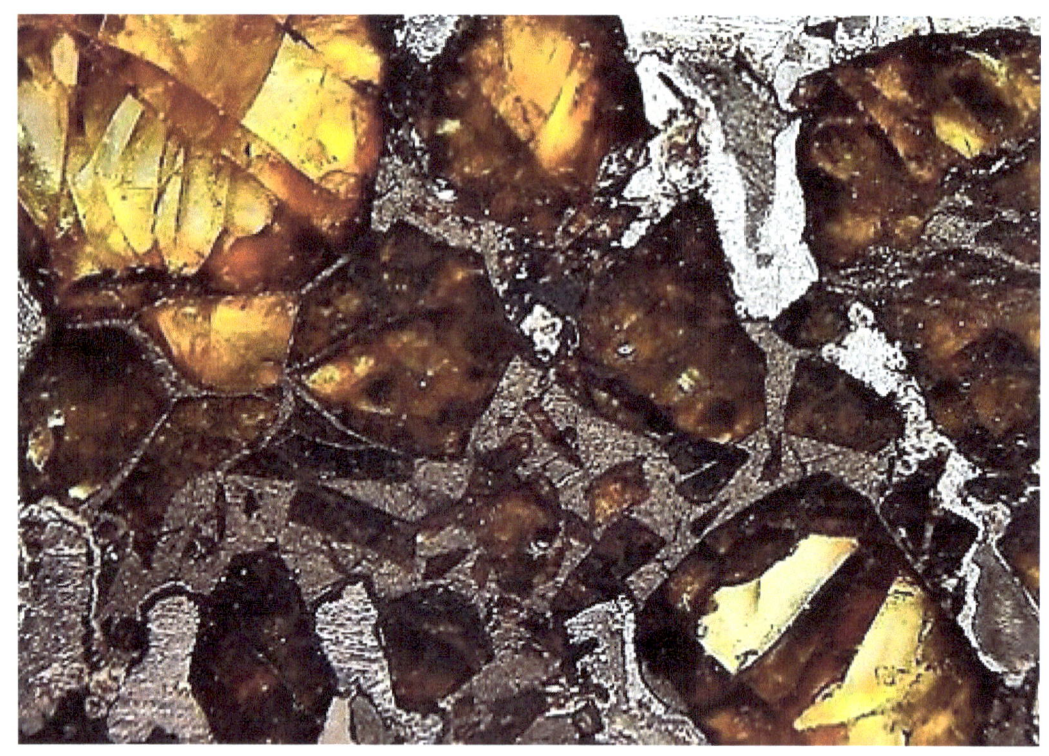

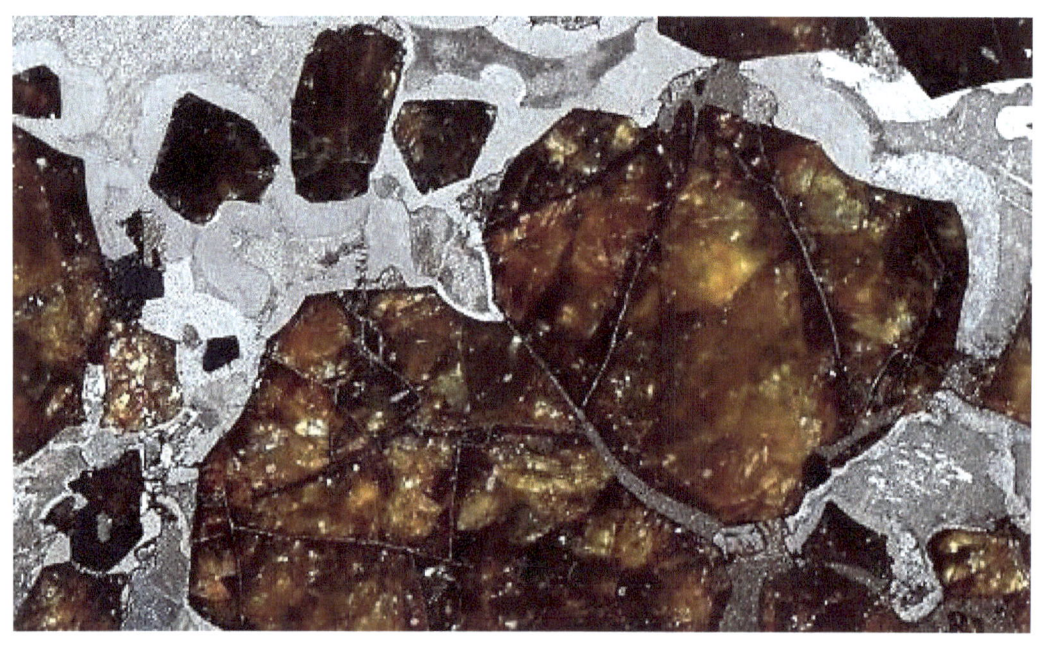

BRENHAM

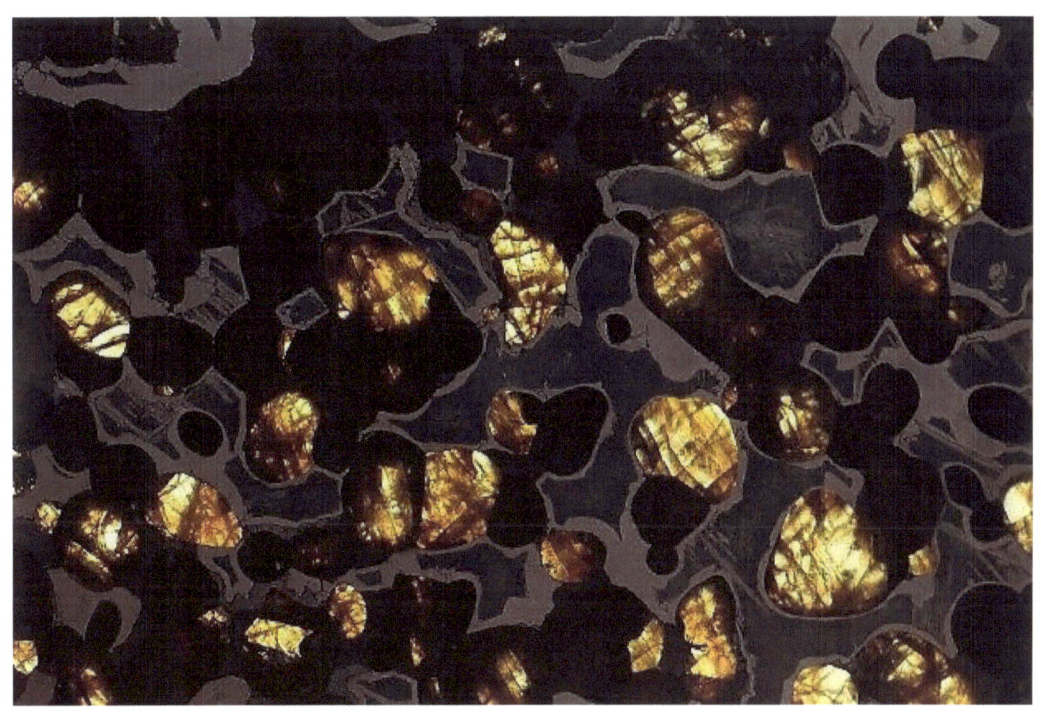

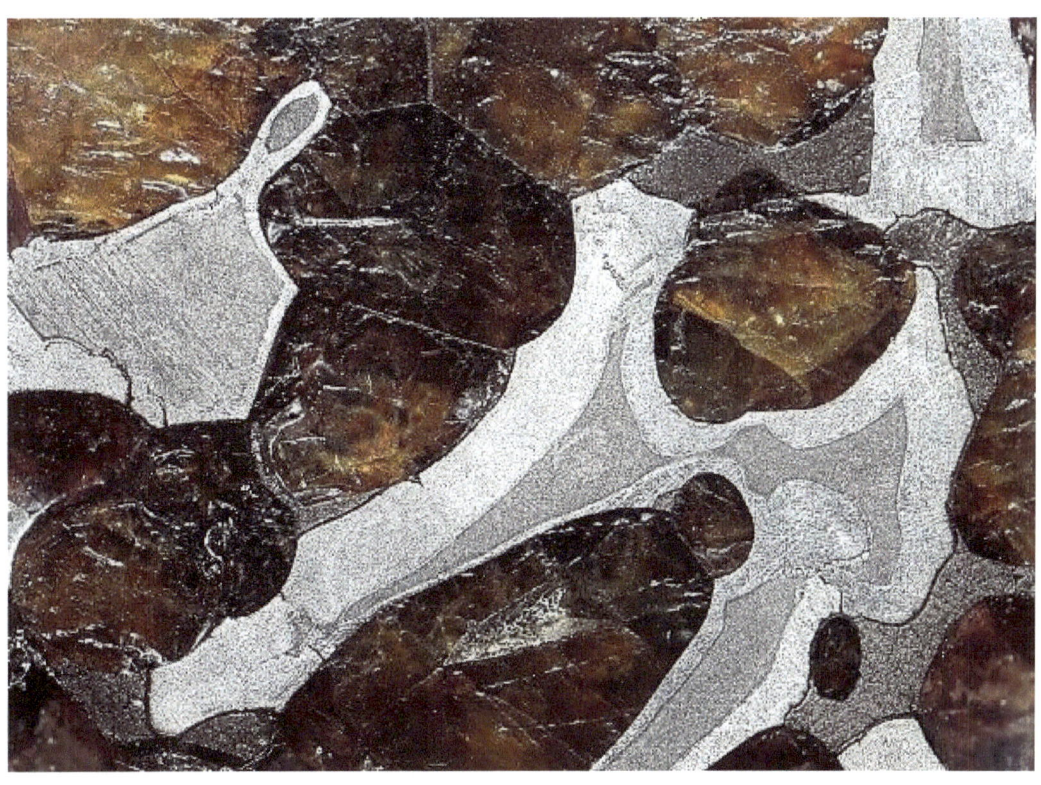

BRENHAM

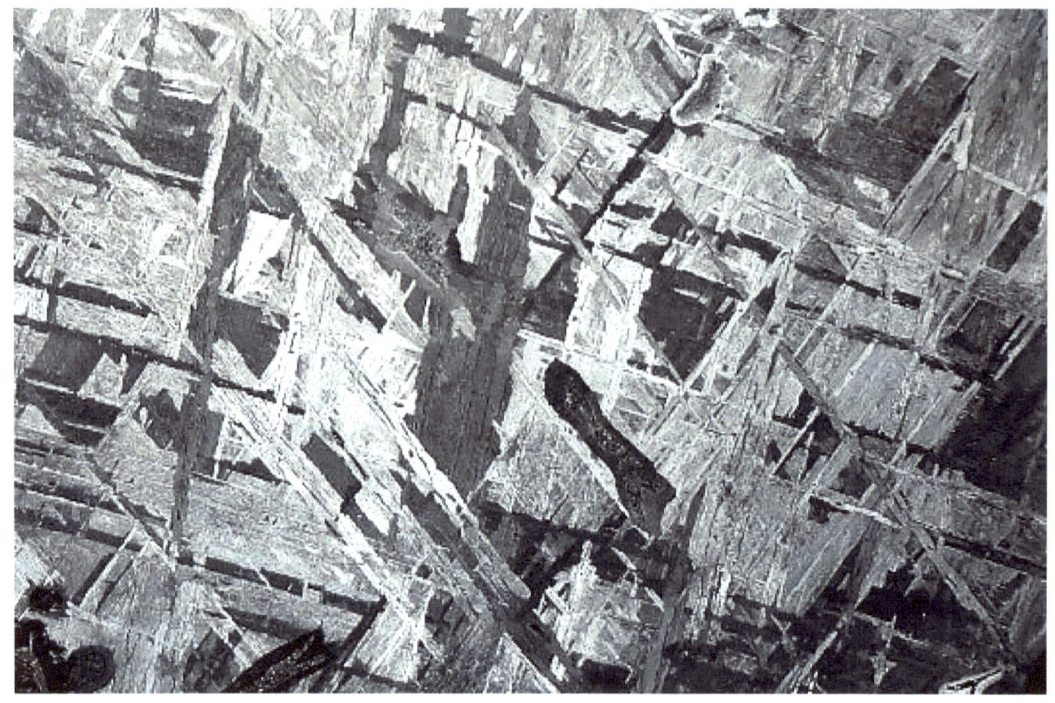

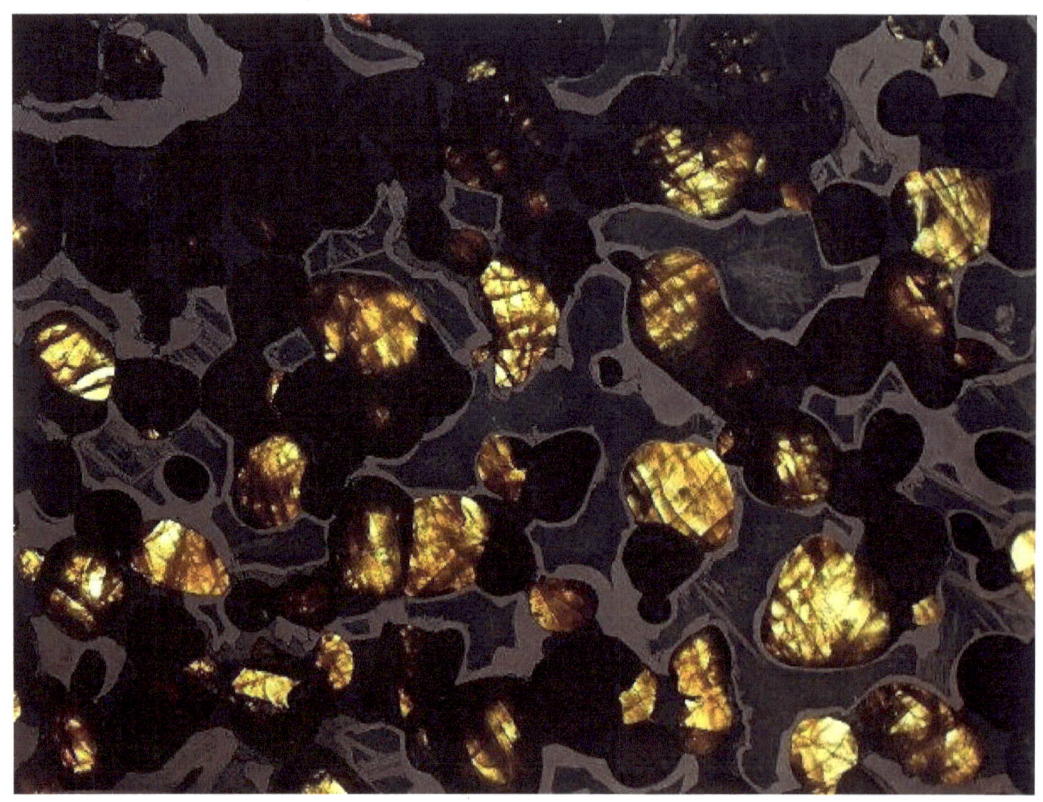

CALAMA 005

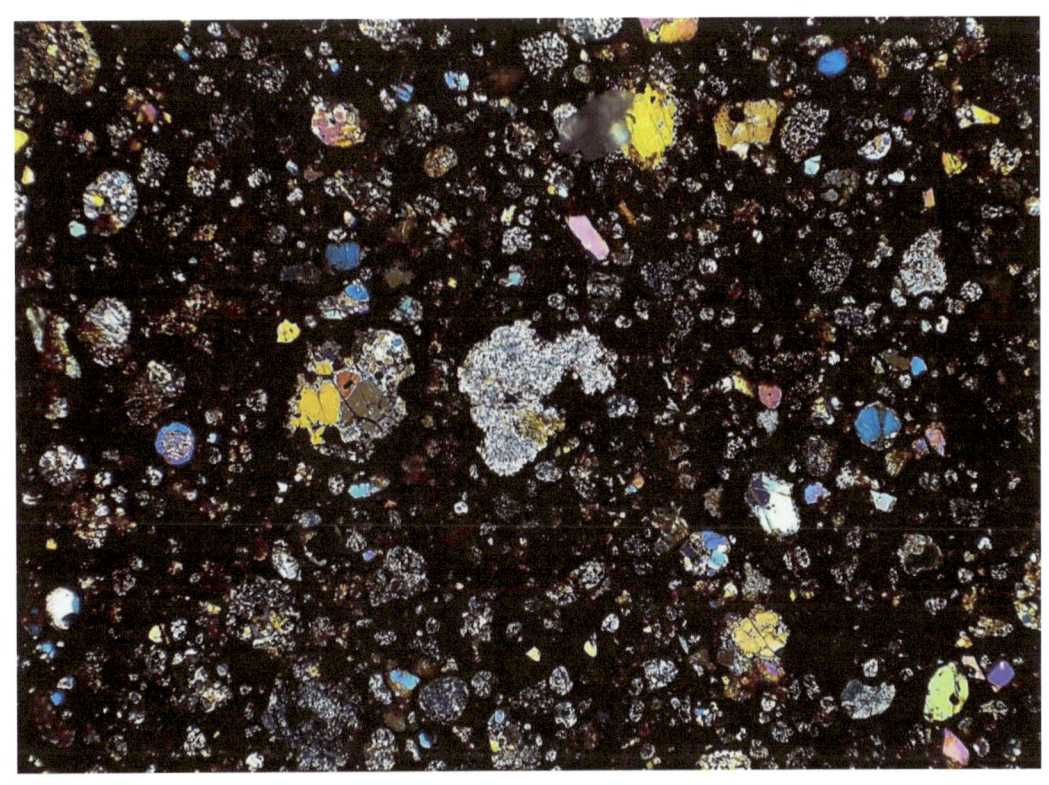

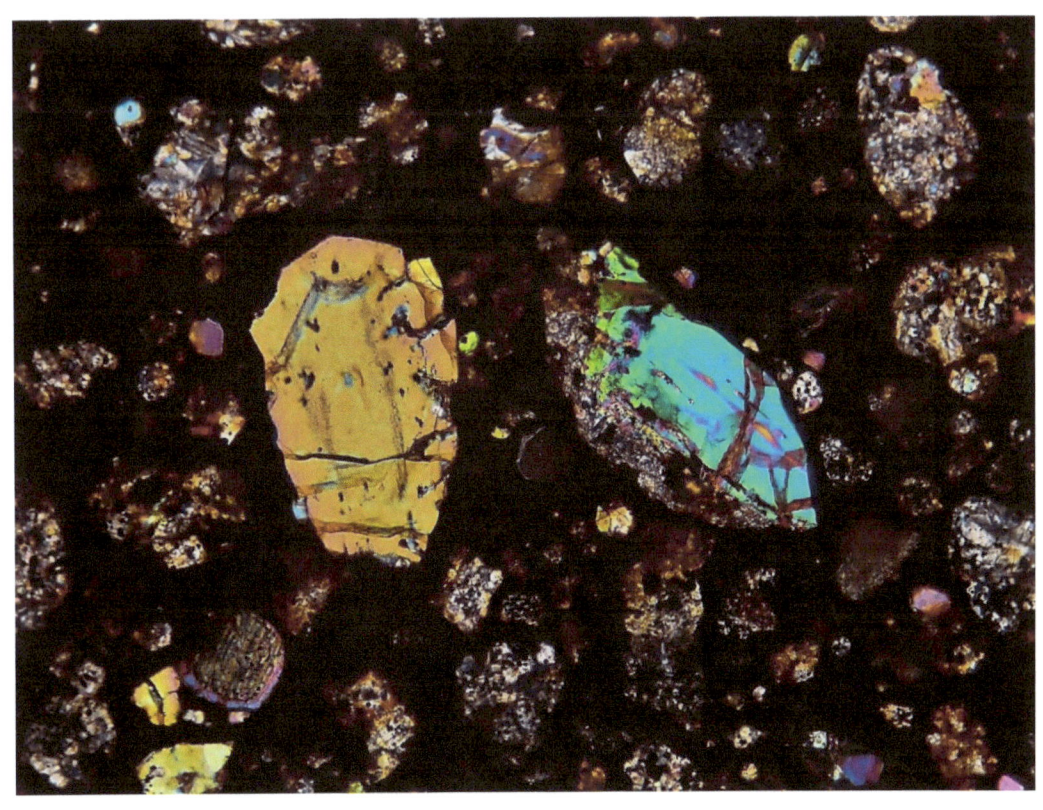

CALAMA 005

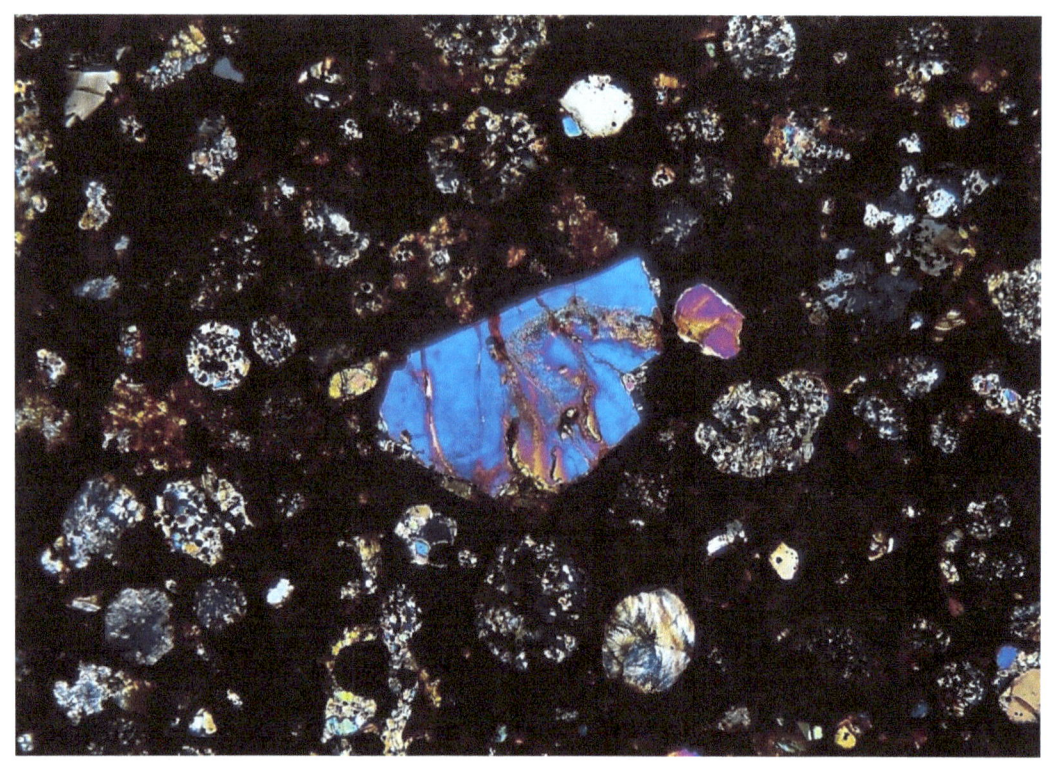

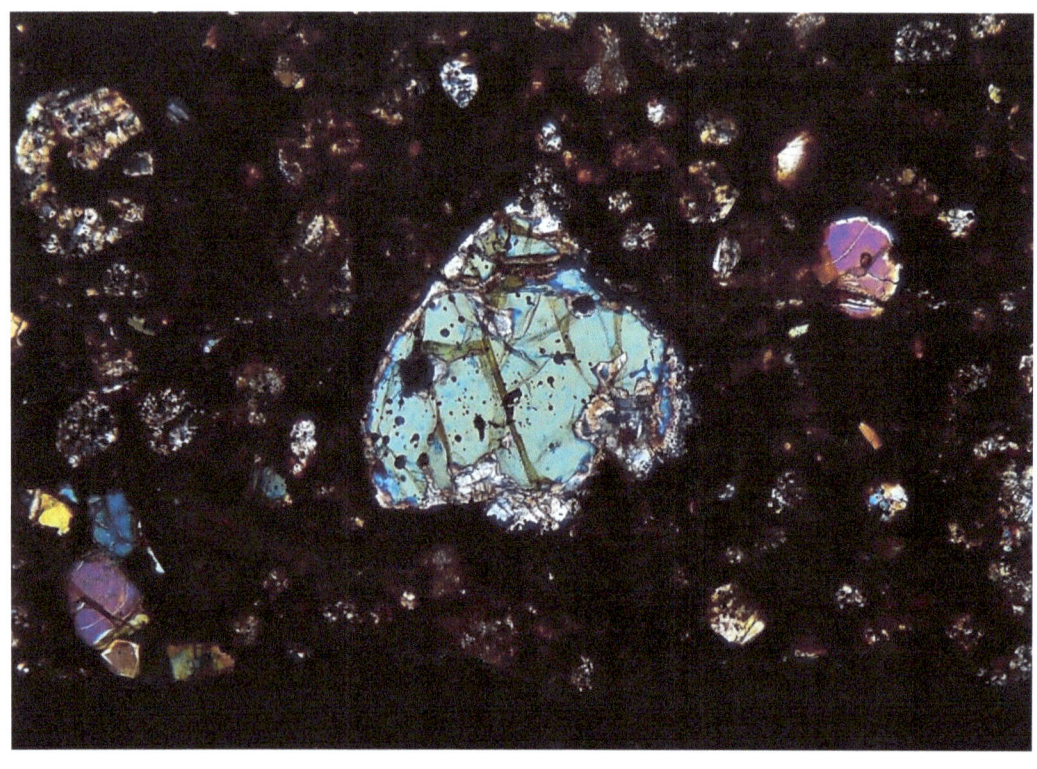

CALAMA 006

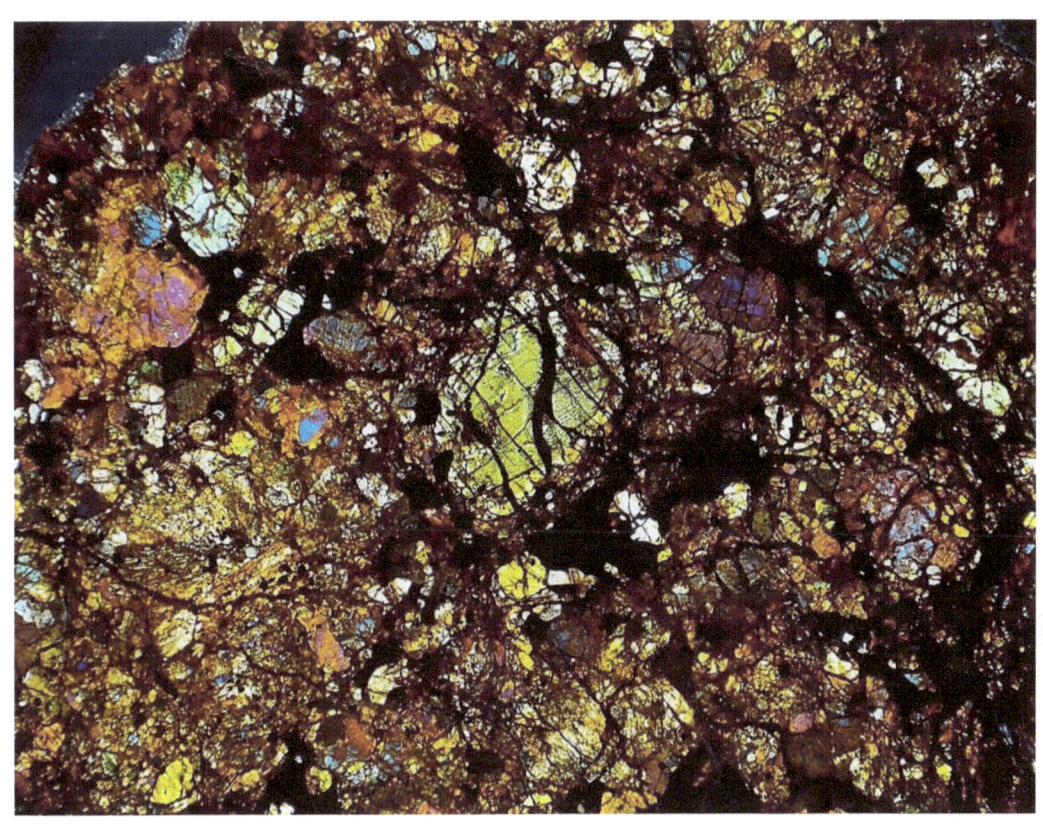

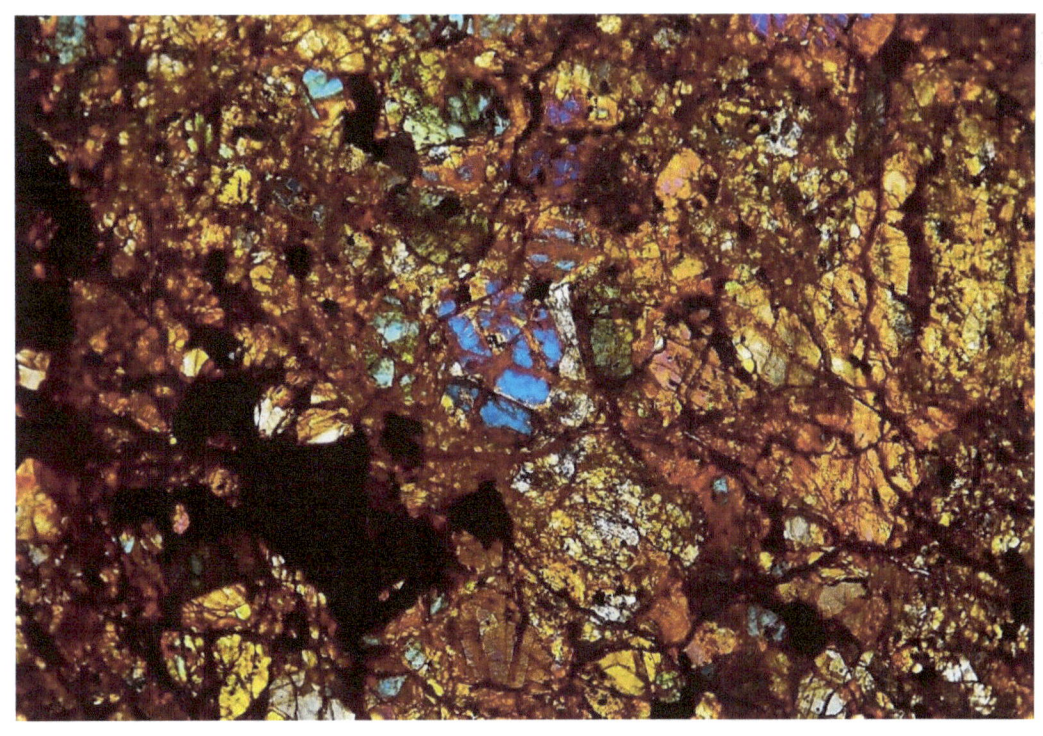

CALAMA 006

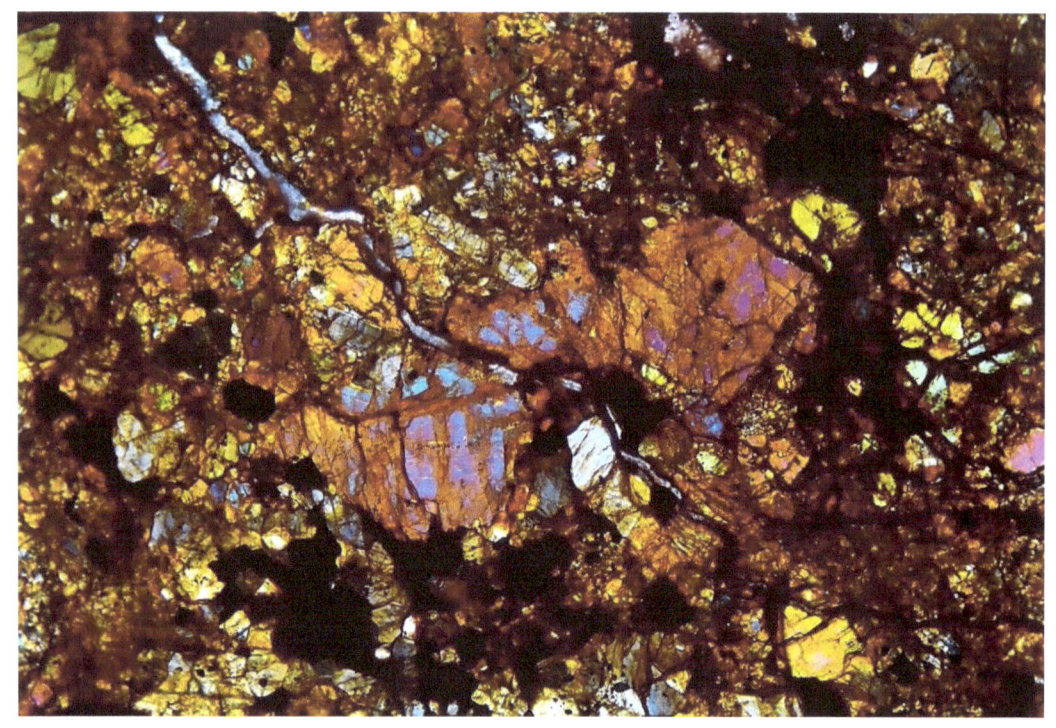

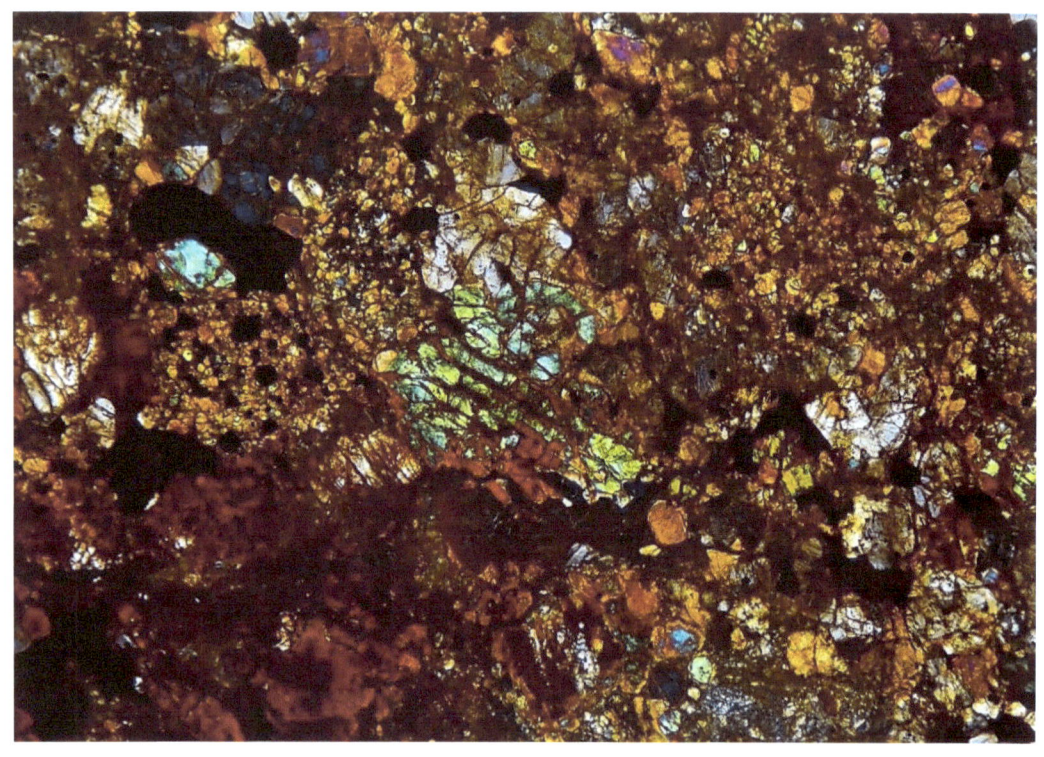

CALAMA 020

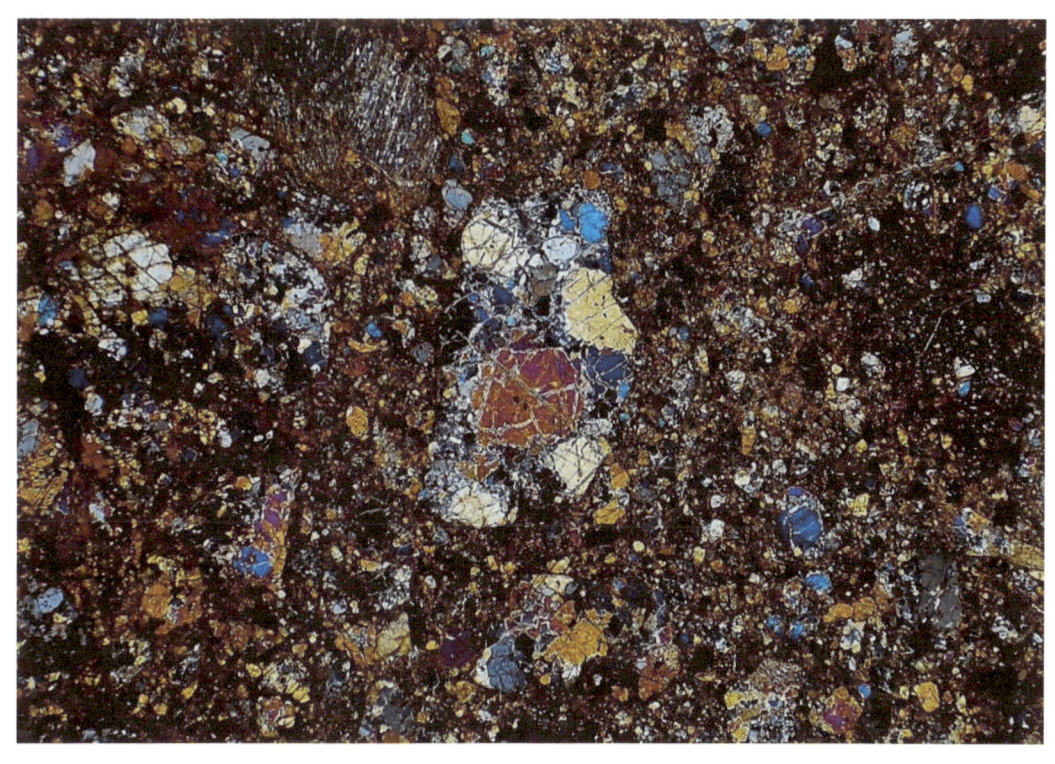

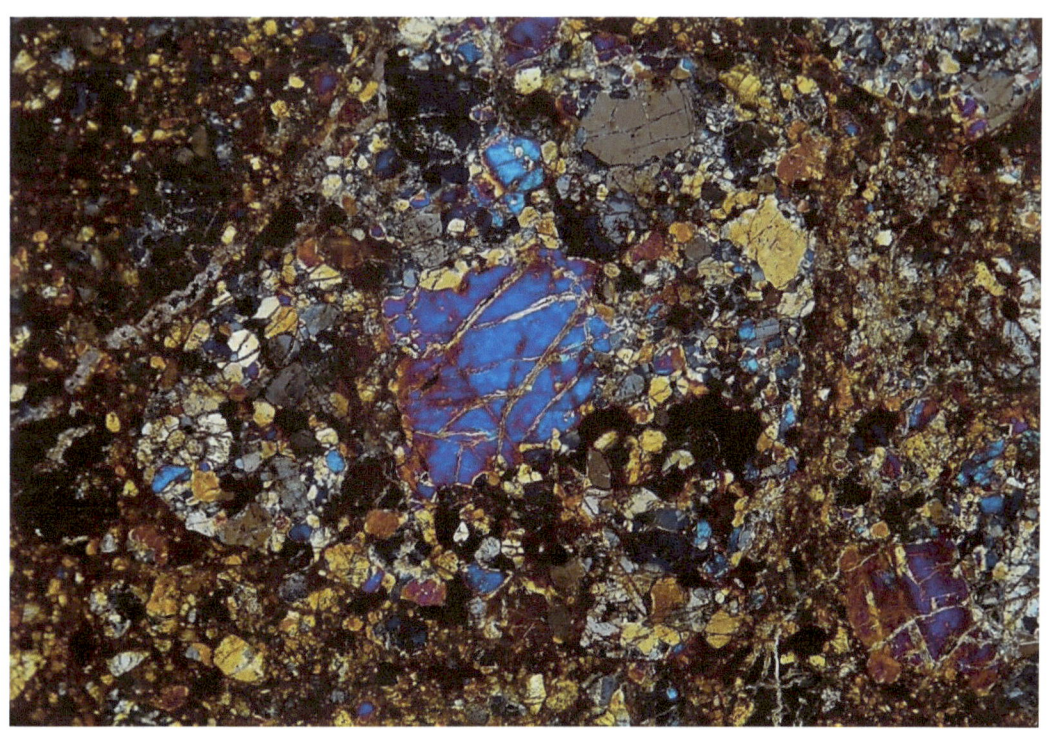

CALAMA 020

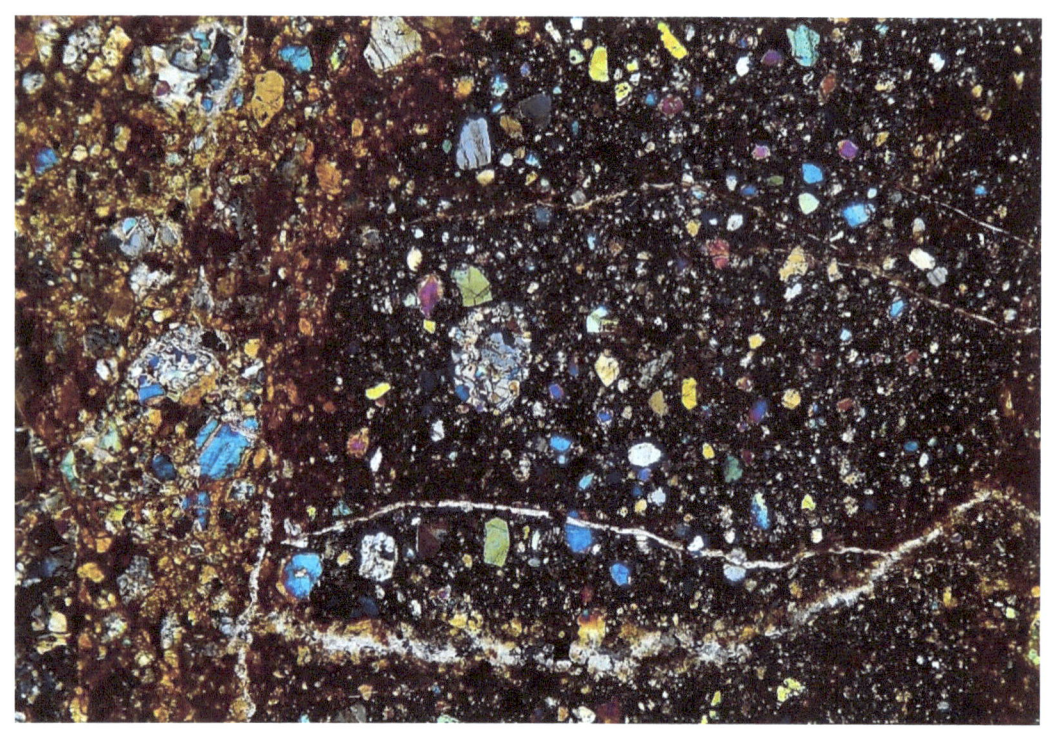

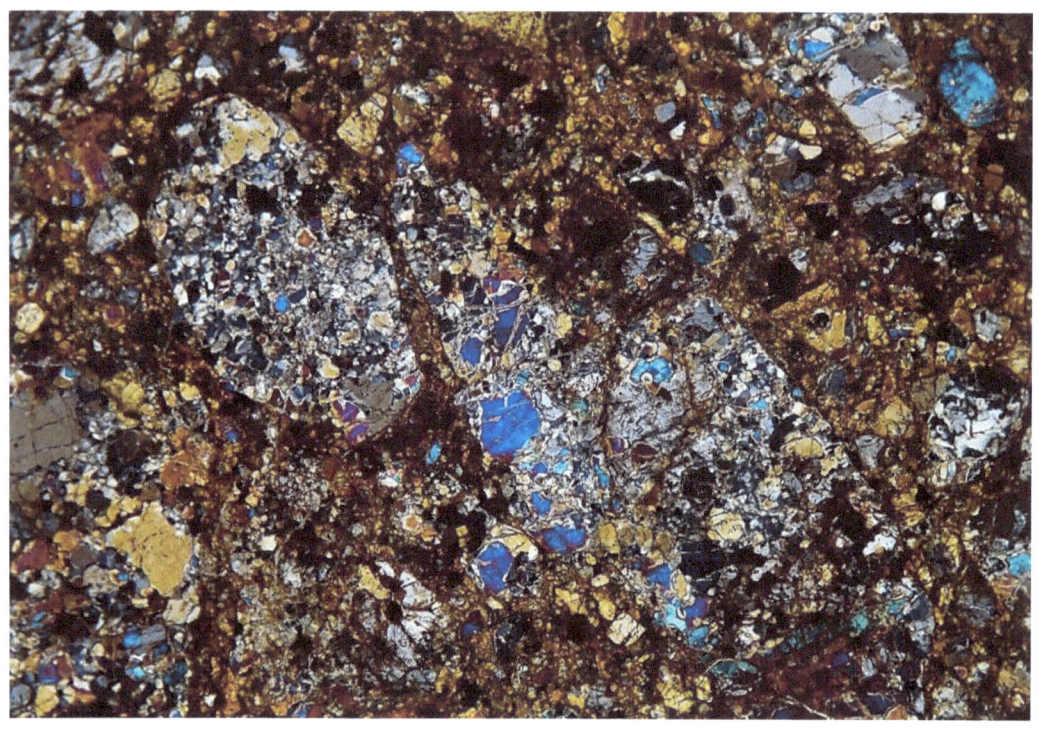

CALAMA 022

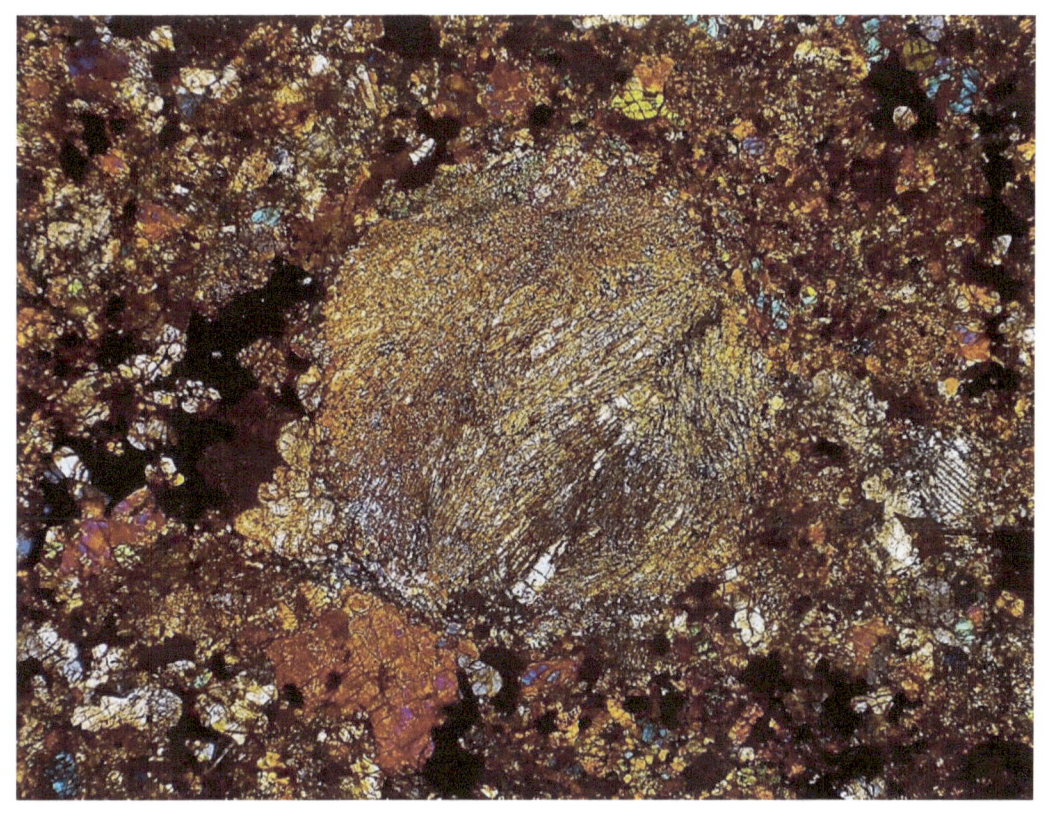

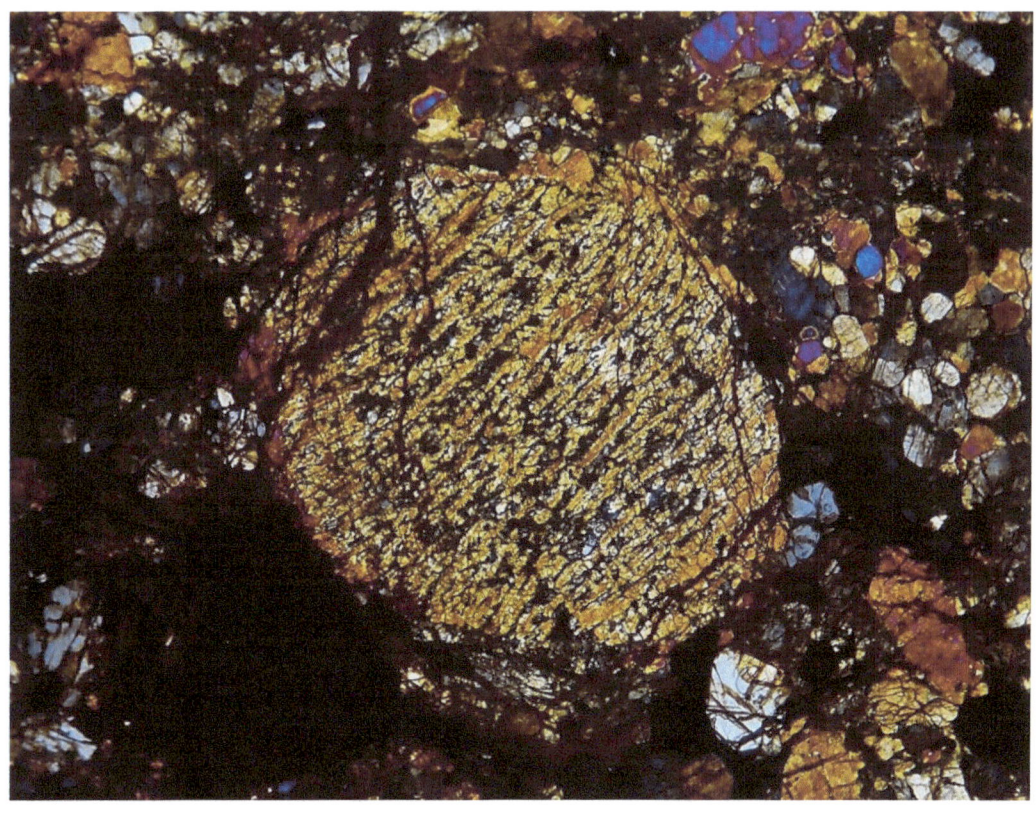

CALAMA 022

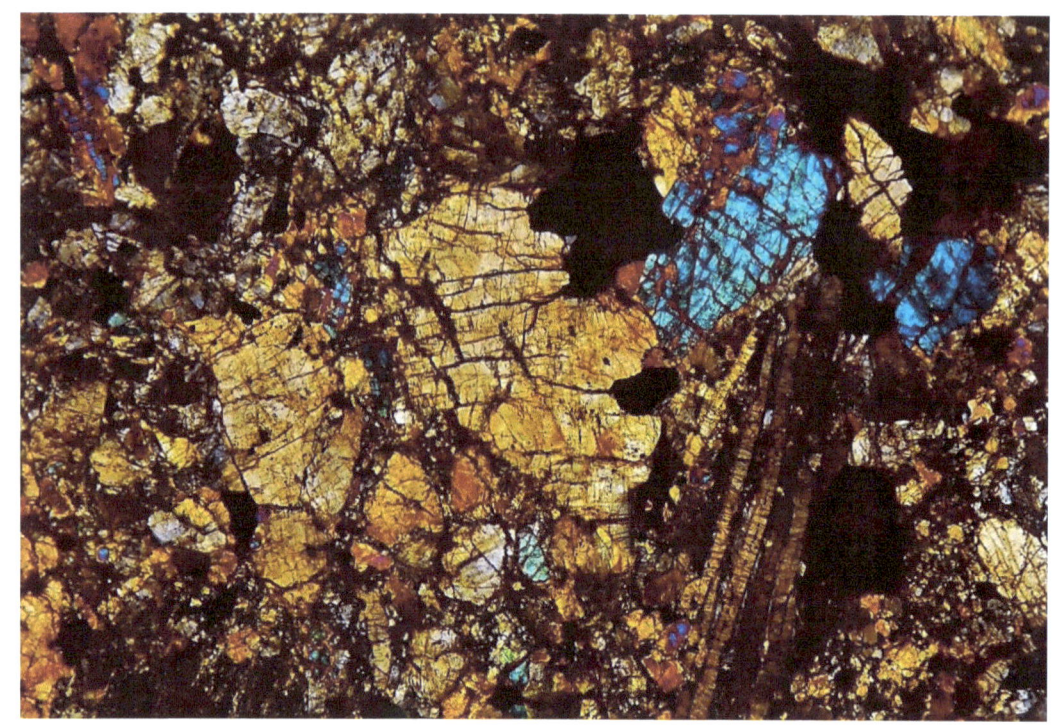

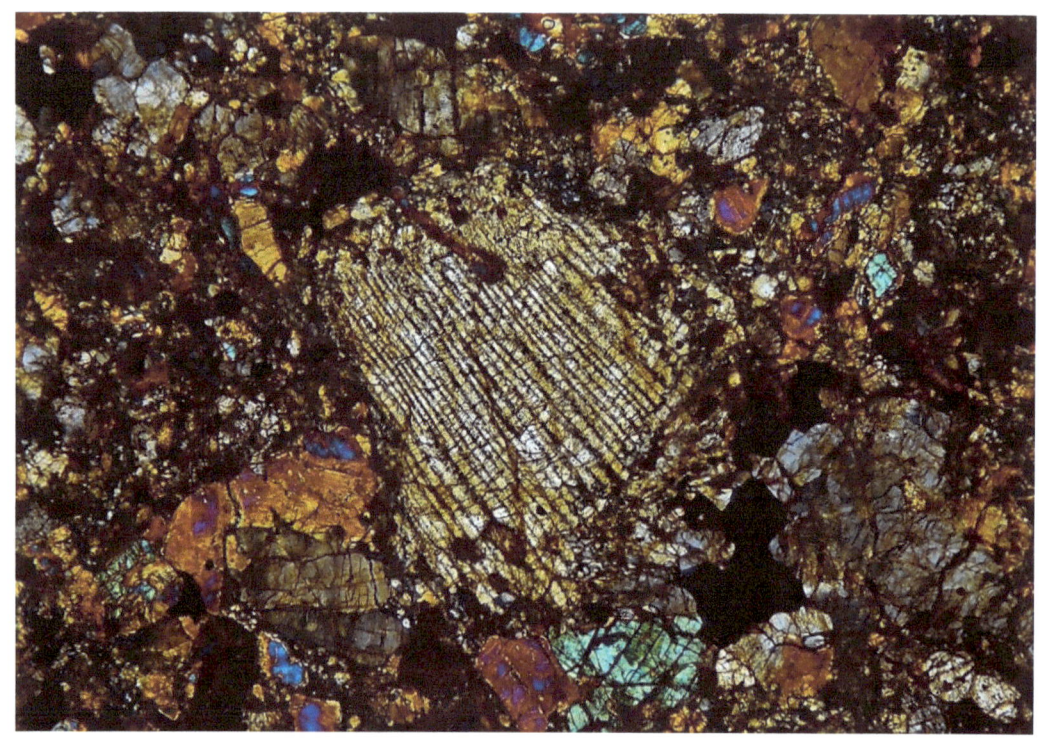

CAMPO DEL CIELO

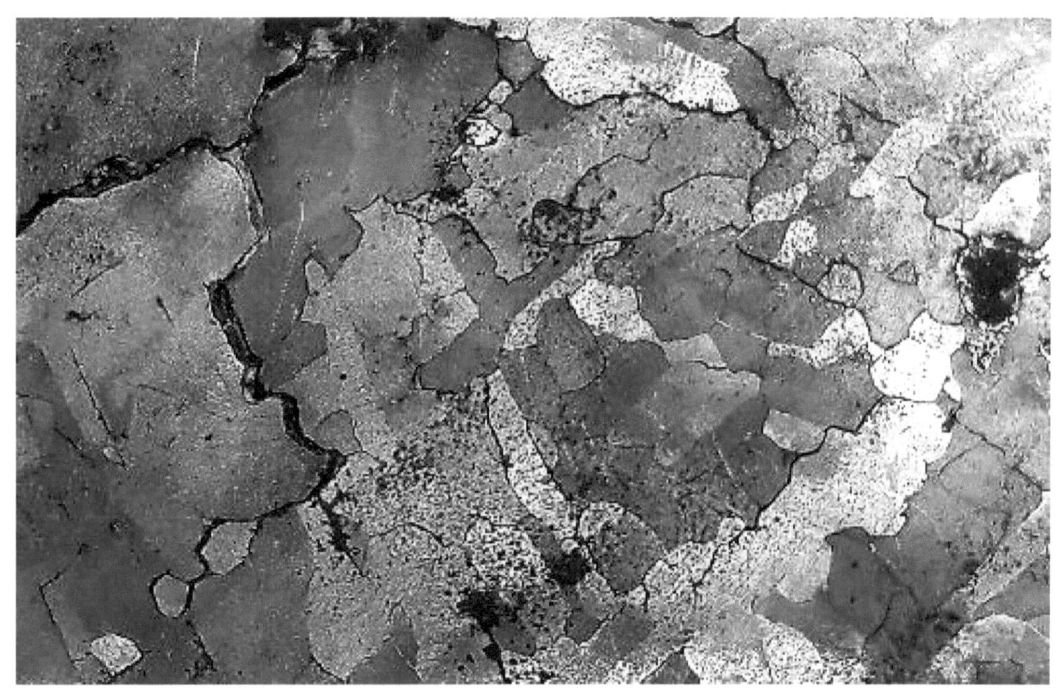

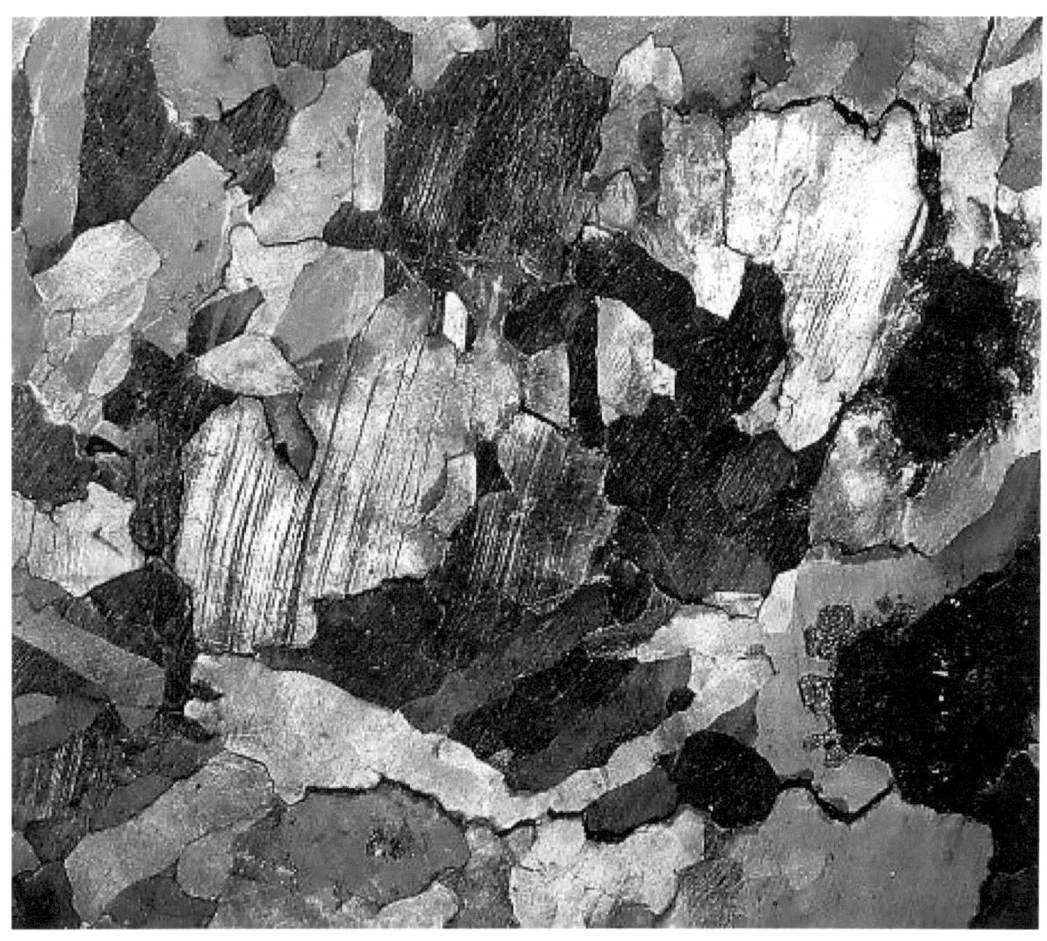

CHUG-CHUG 004

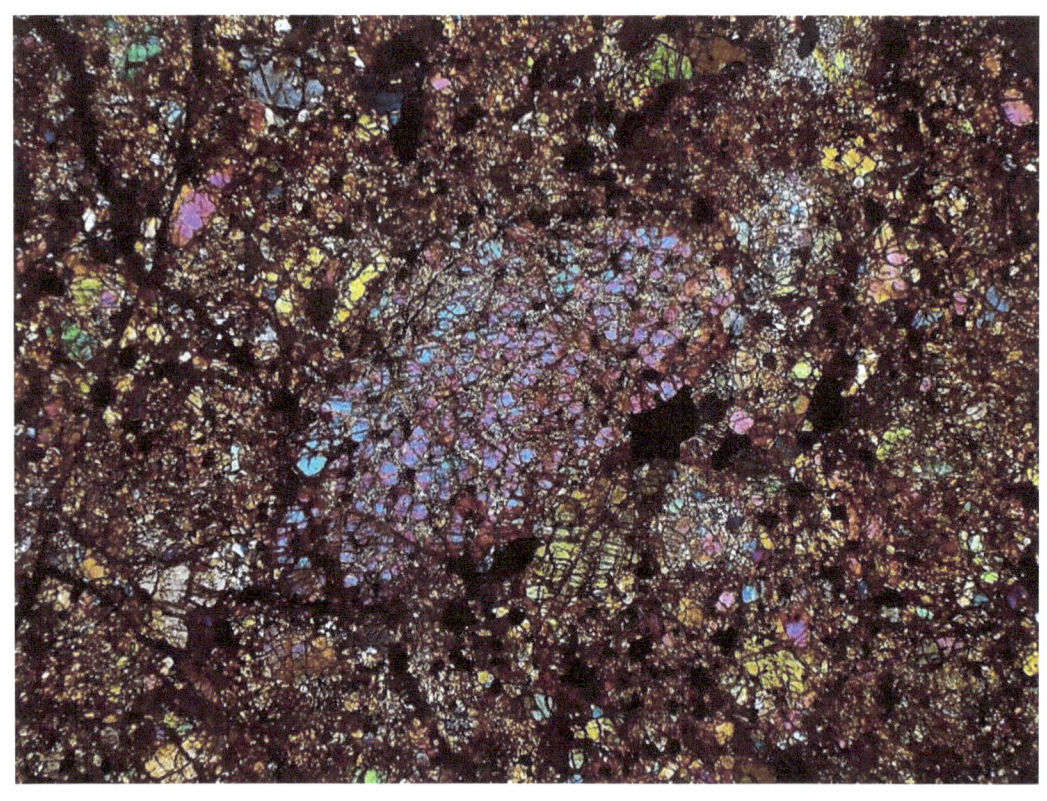

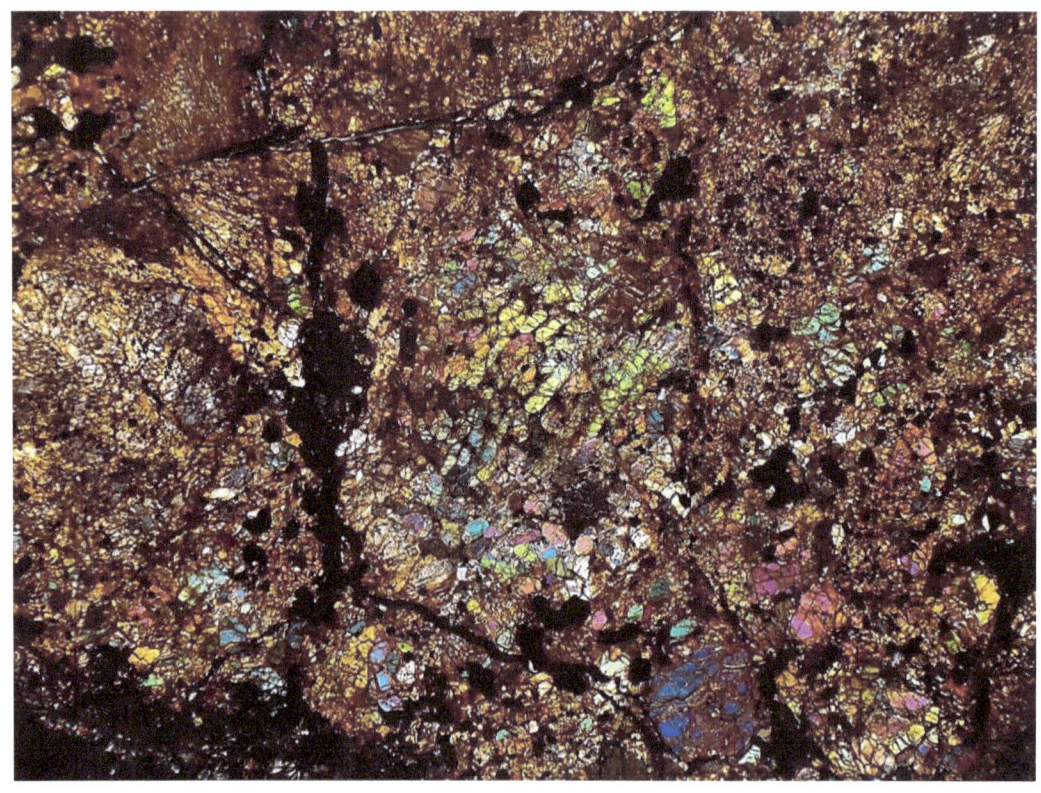

CHUG-CHUG 004

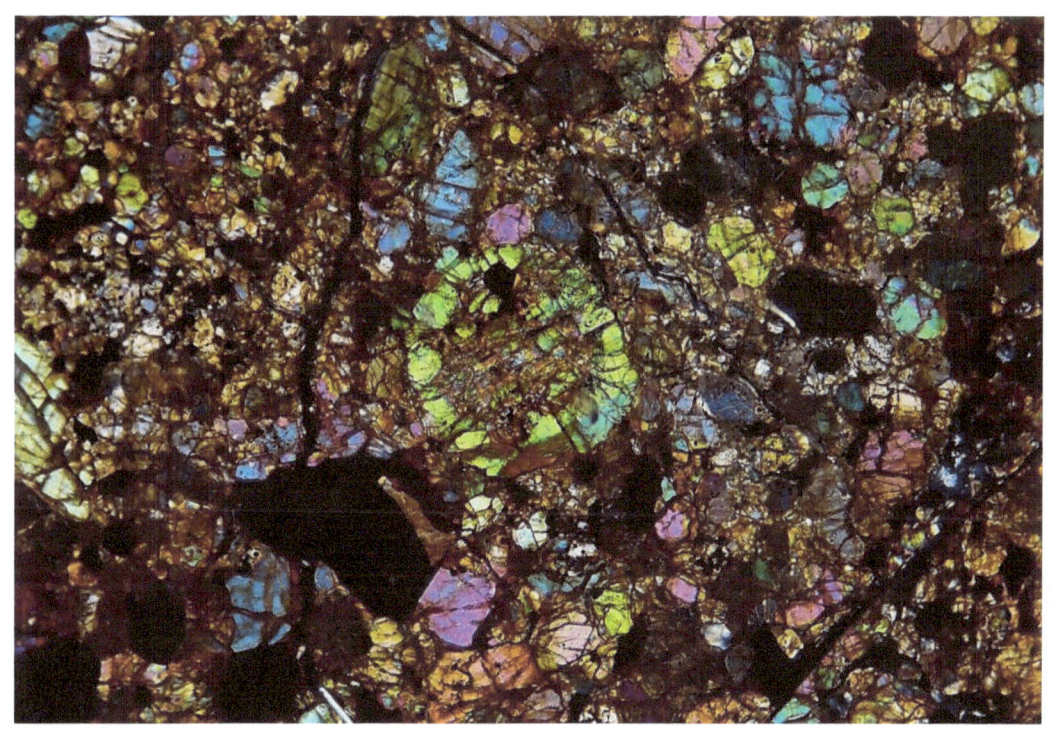

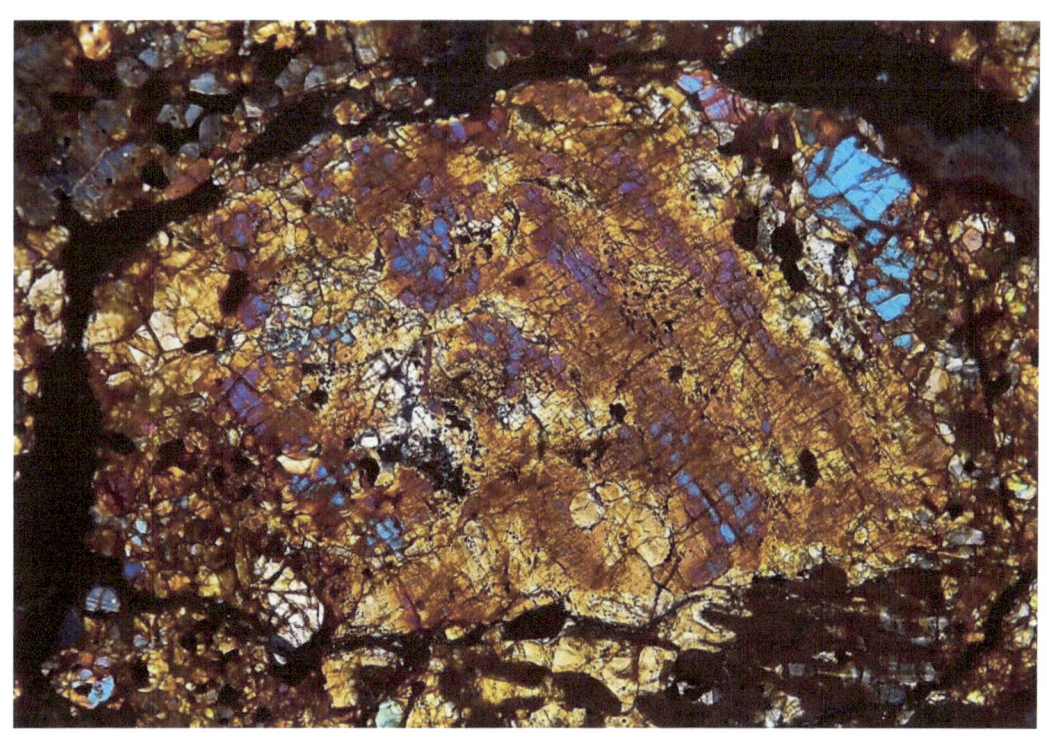

CHUG-CHUG 009

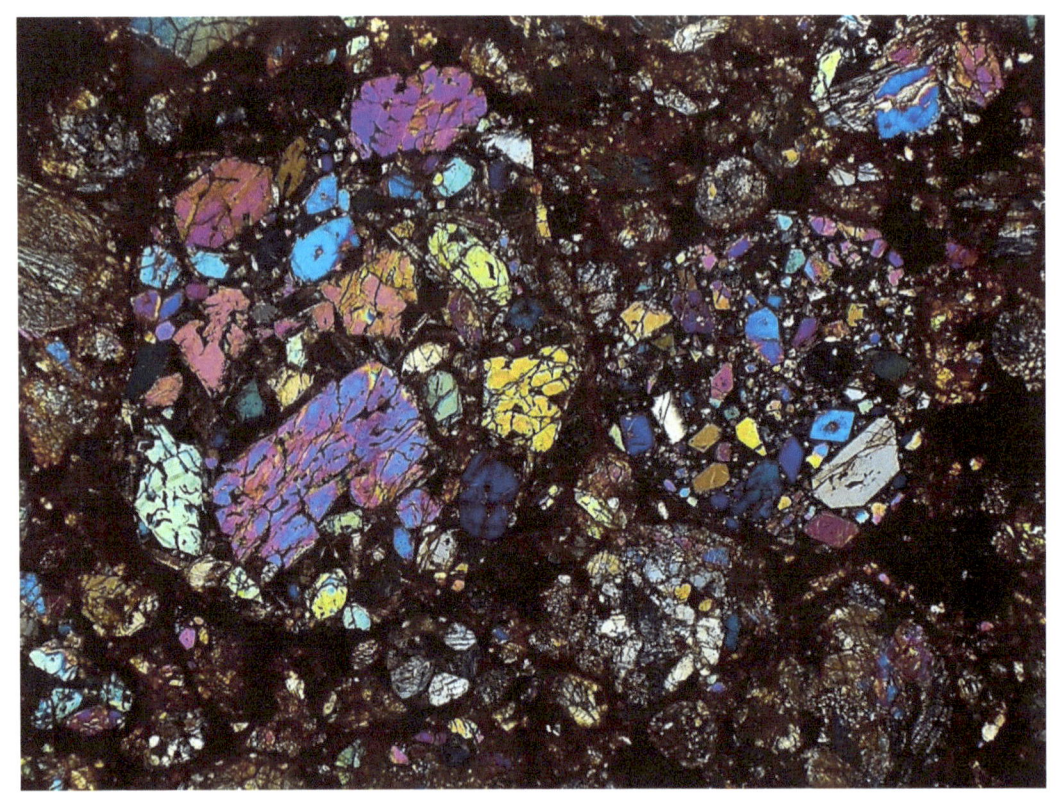

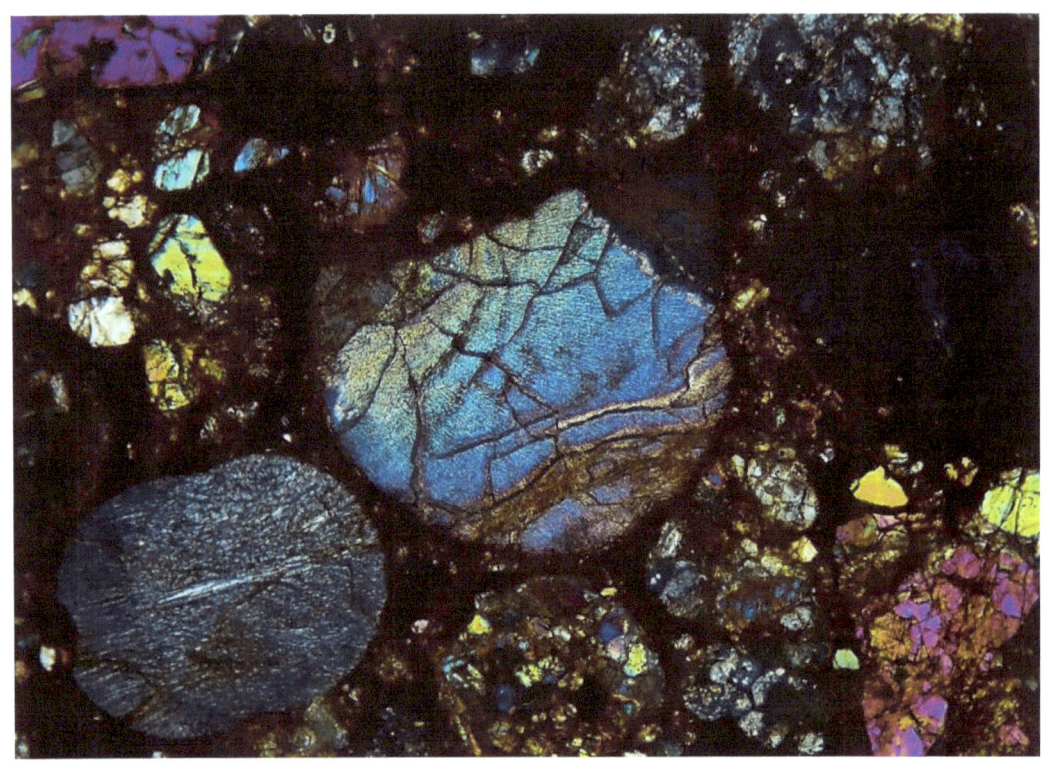

CHUG-CHUG 009

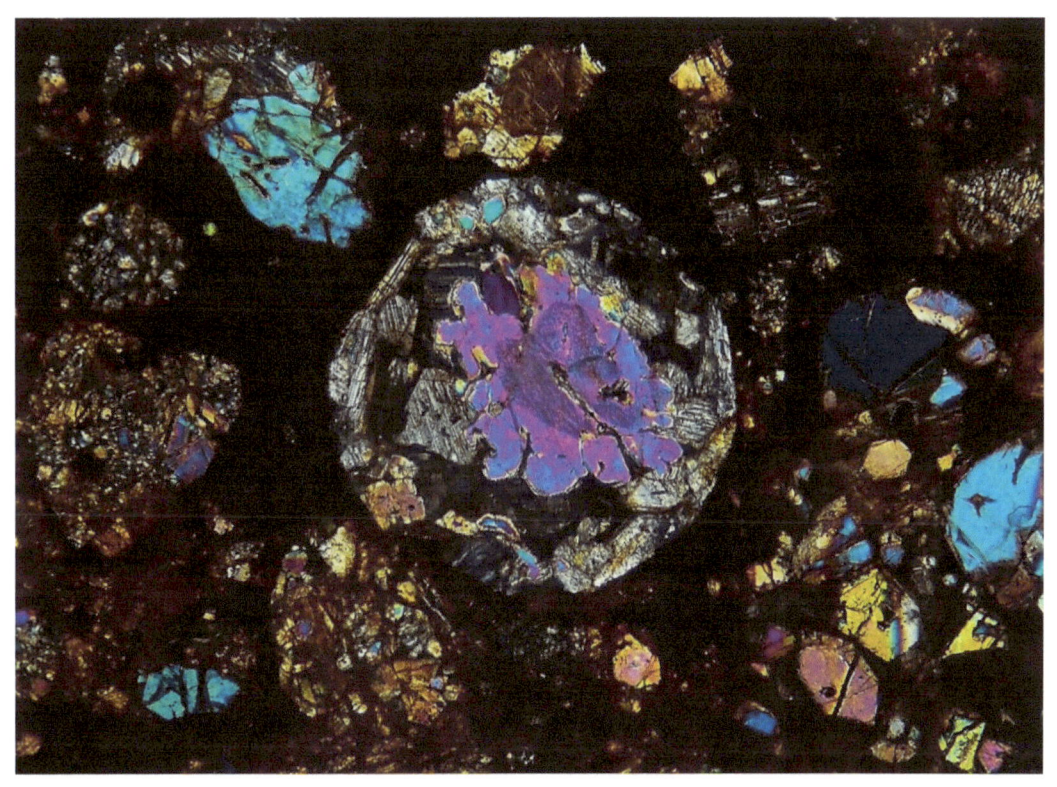

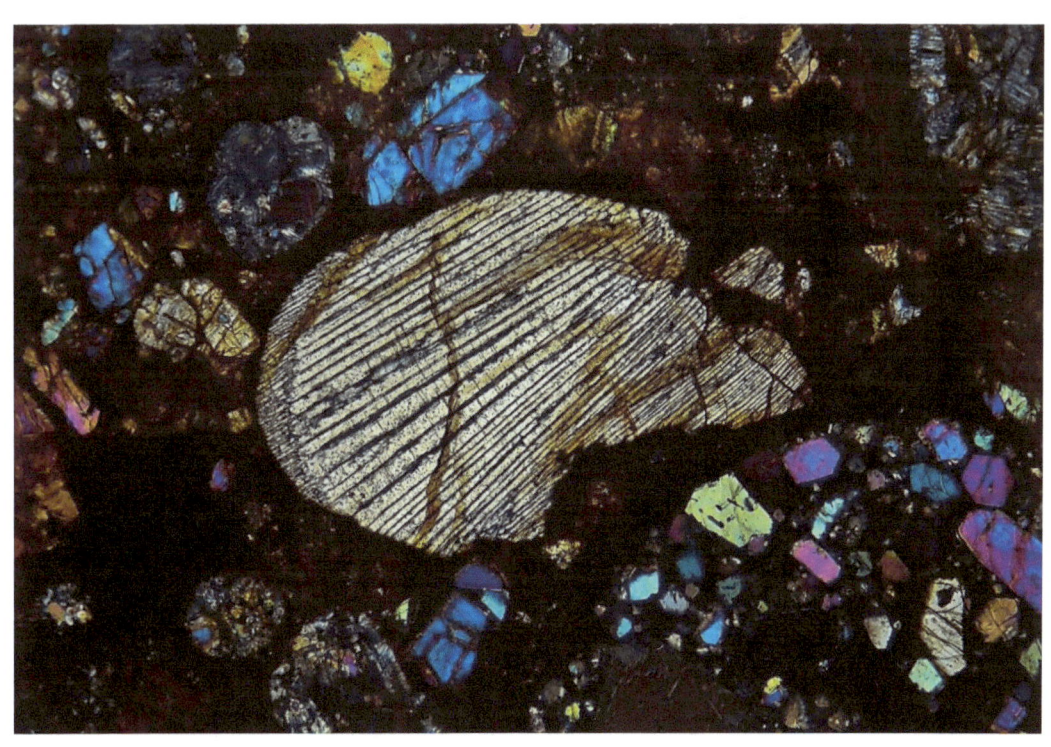

CHUG-CHUG 011

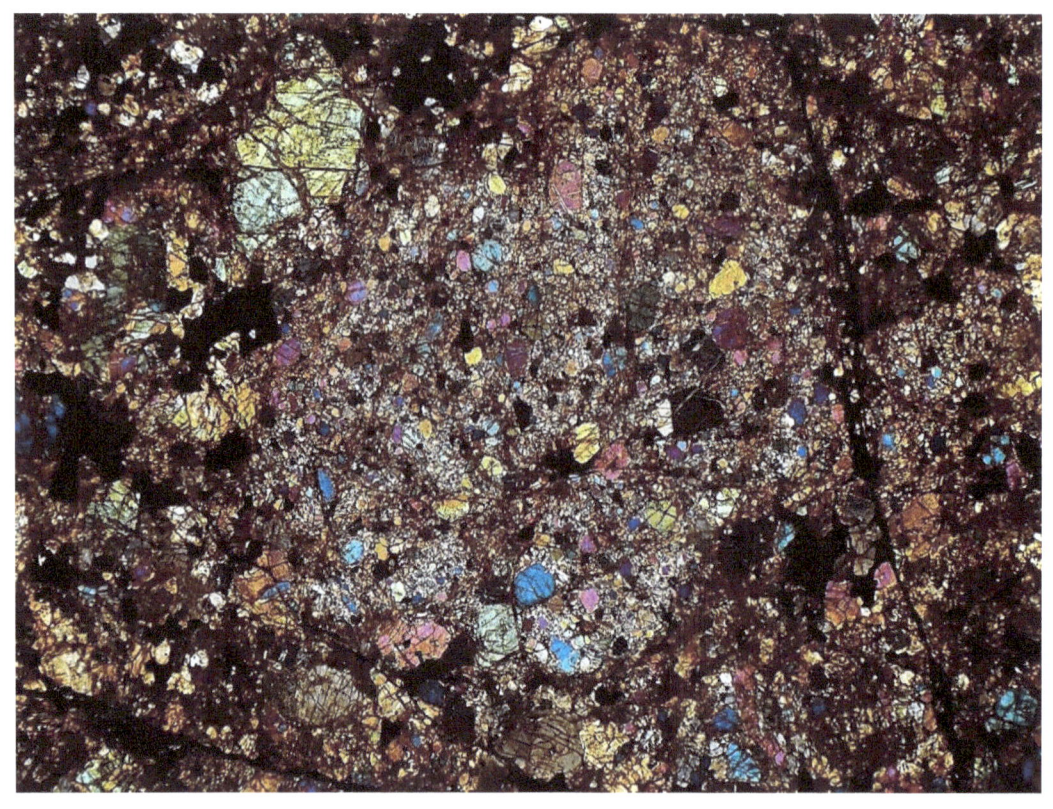

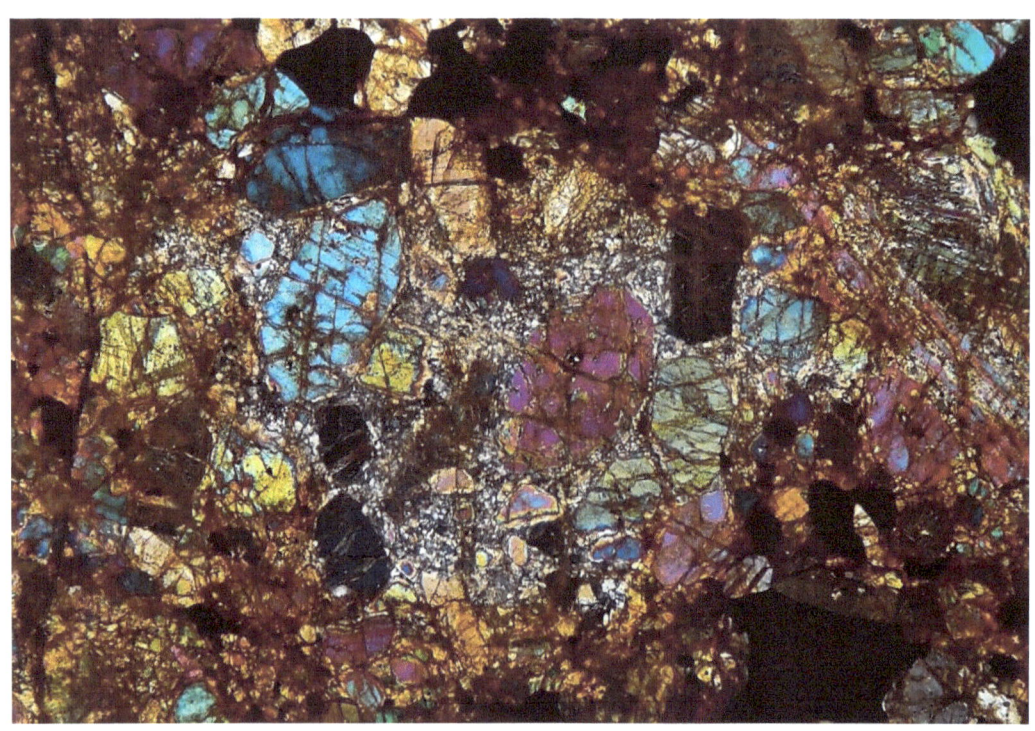

CHUG-CHUG 011

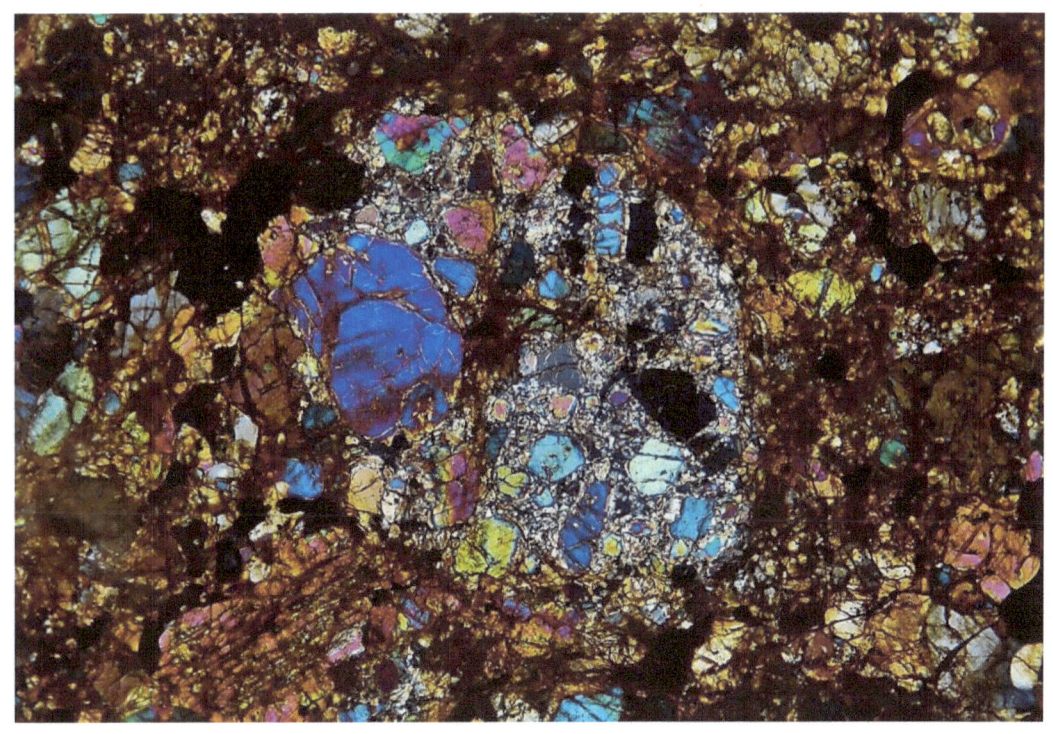

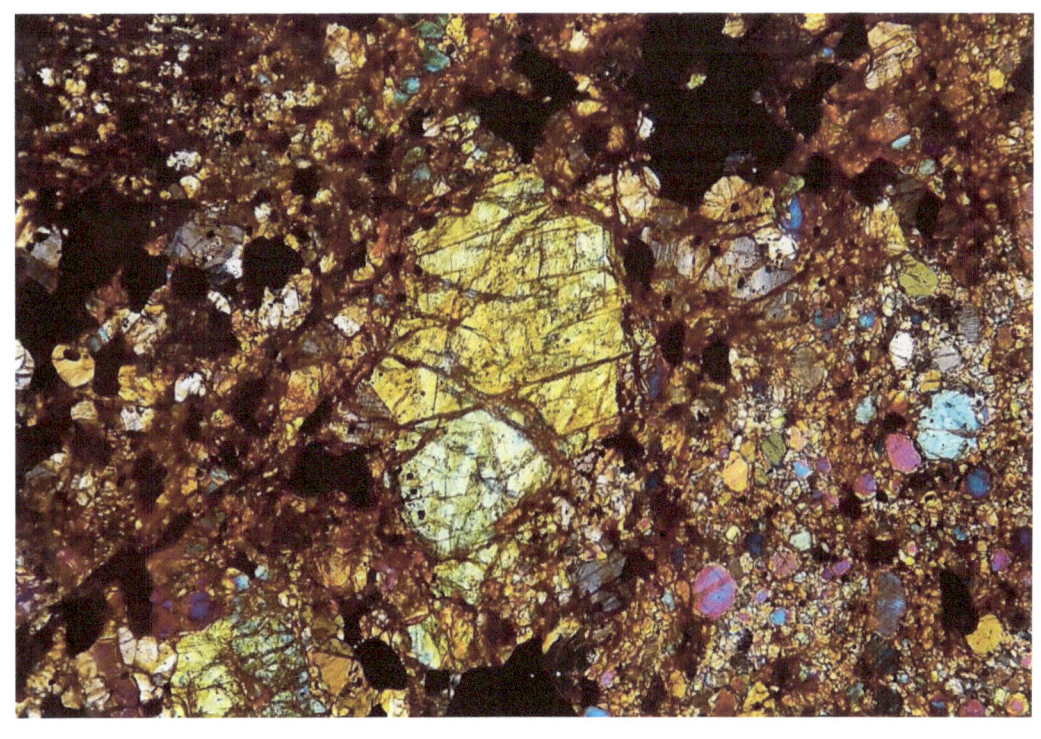

CLARENDON

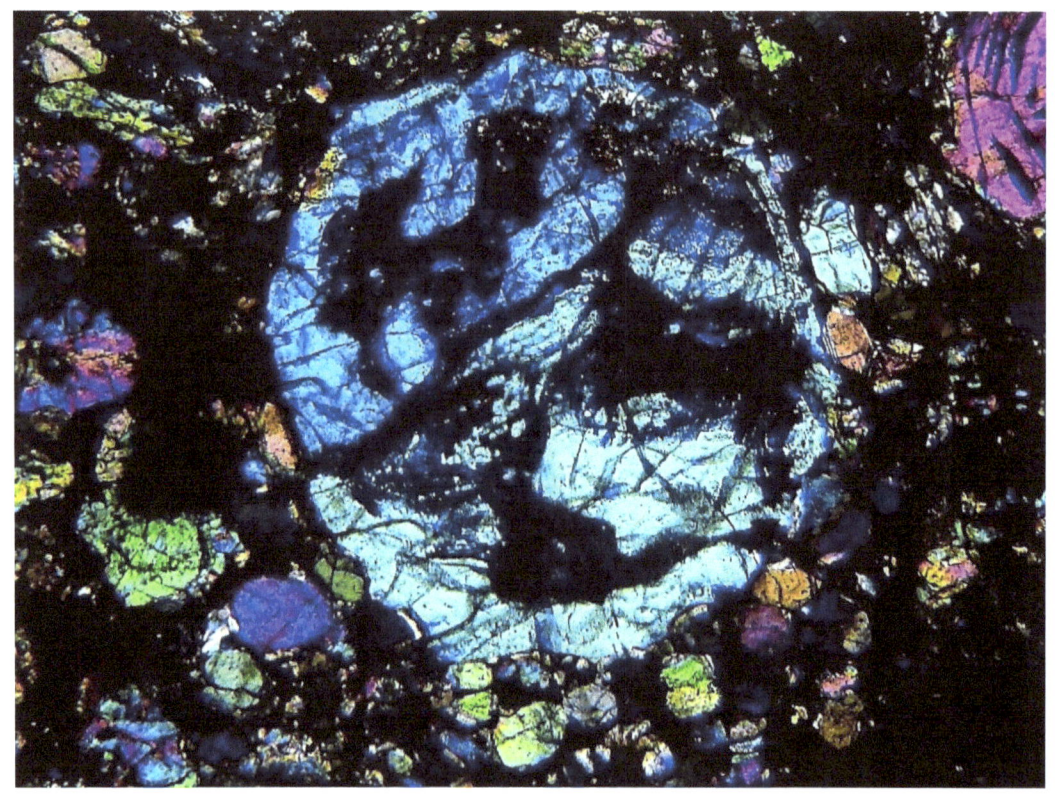

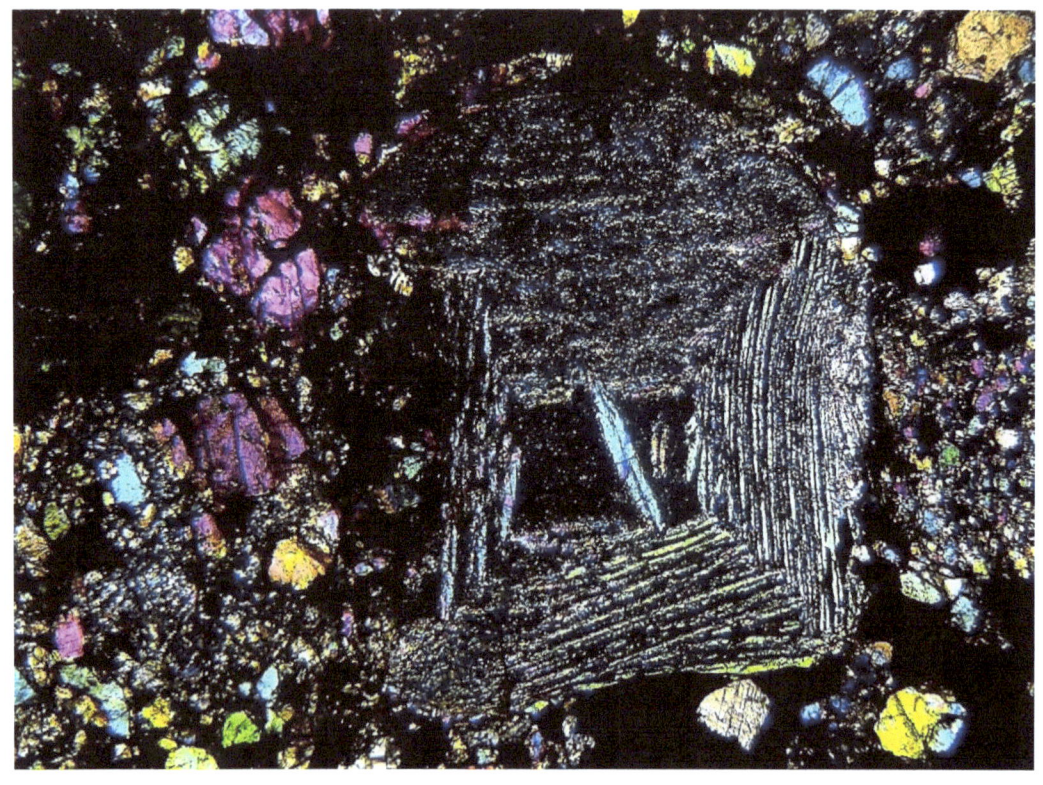

CLARENDON

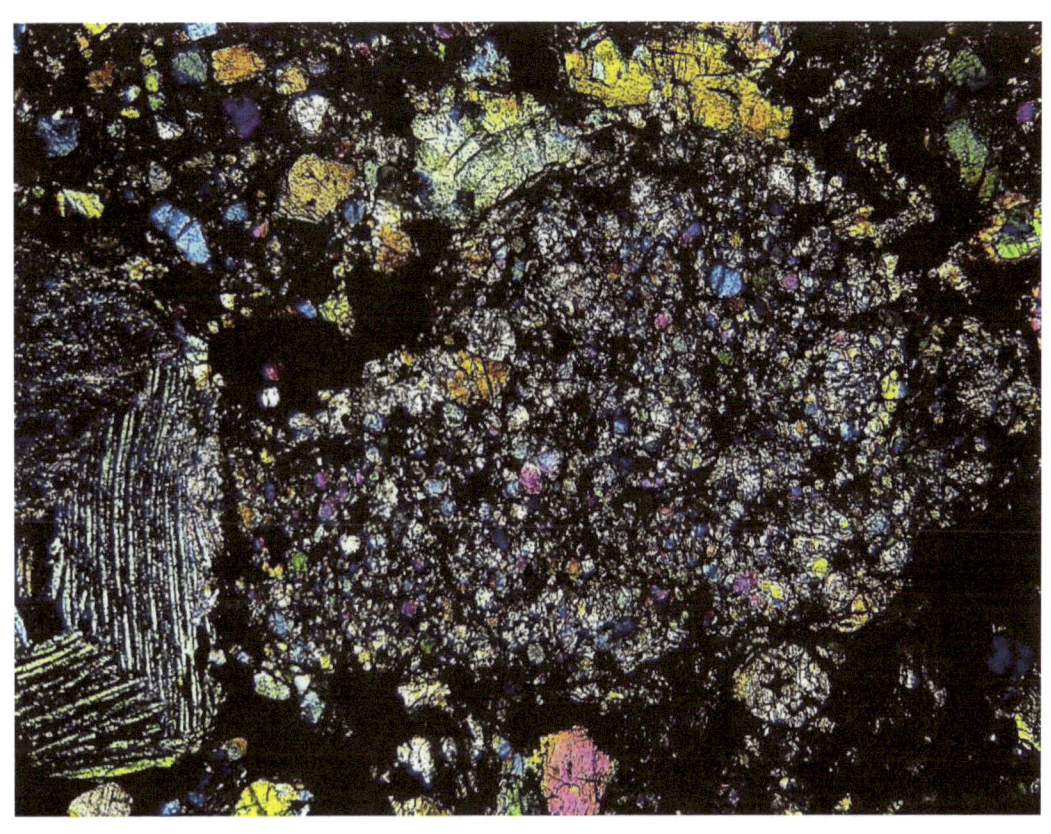

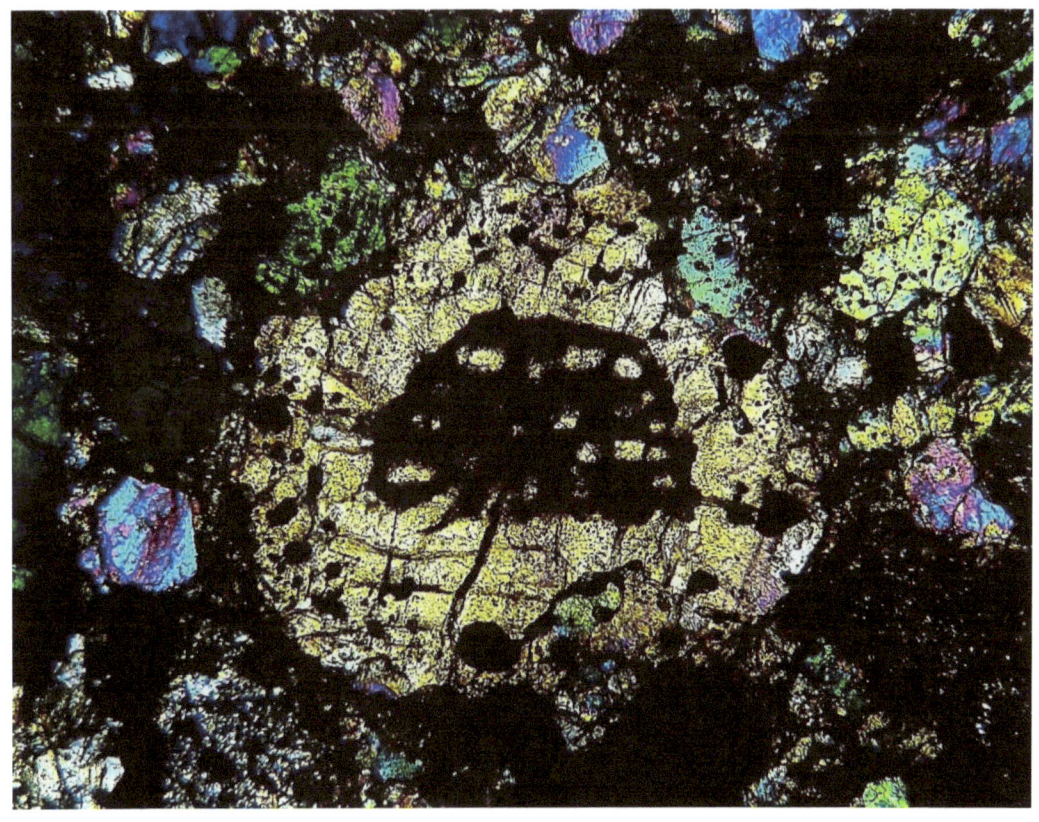

CLARENDON

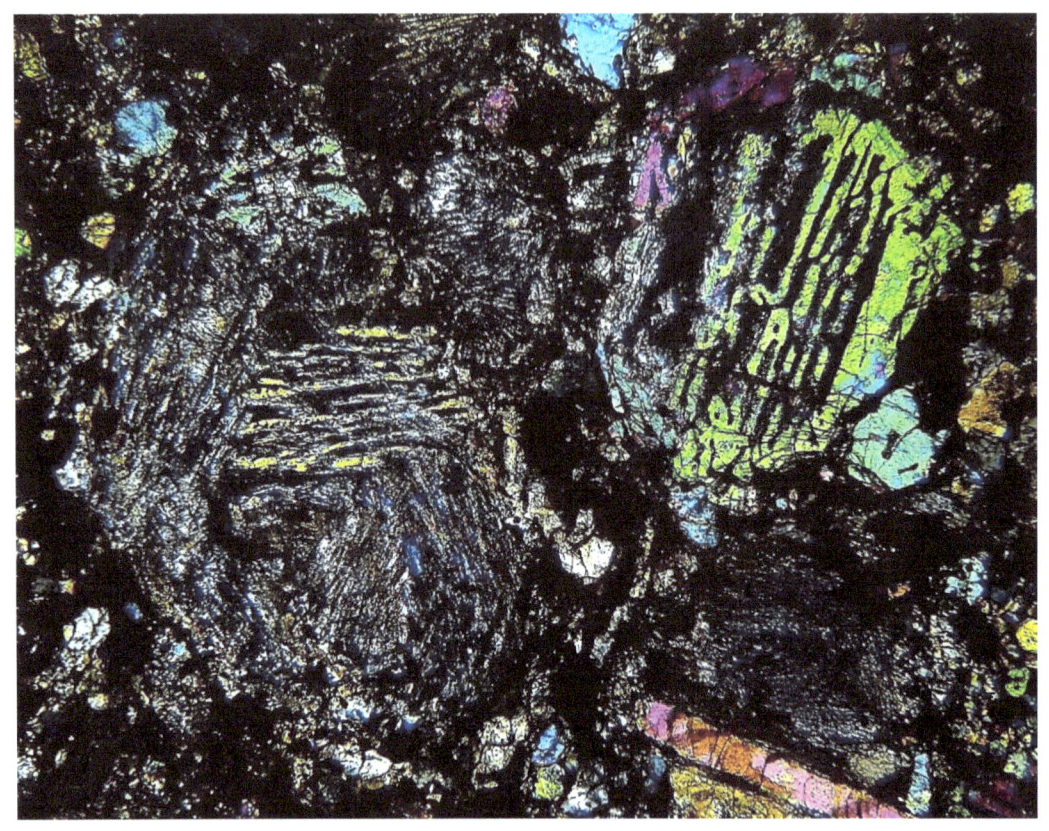

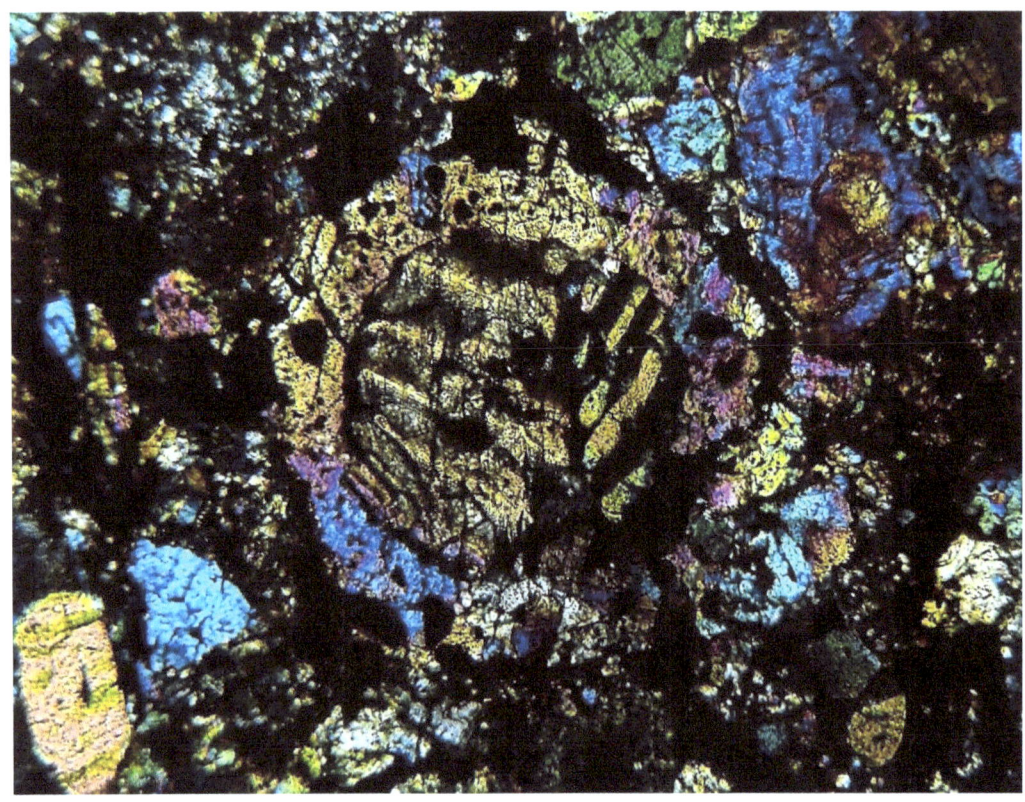

CLARENDON

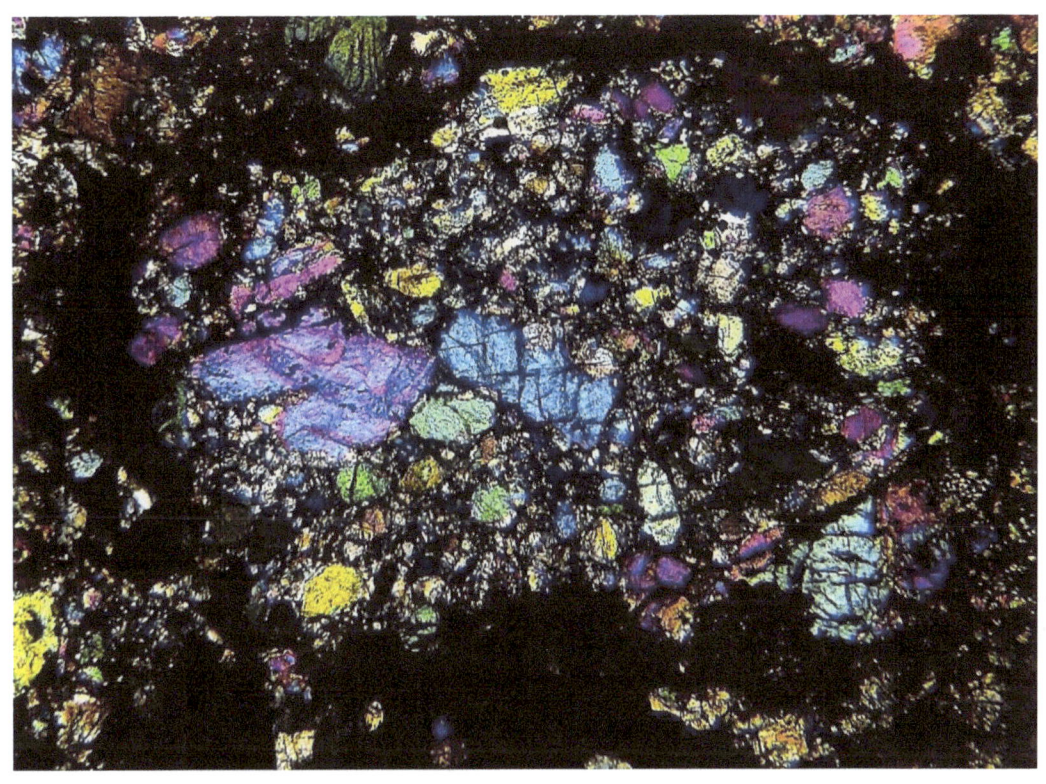

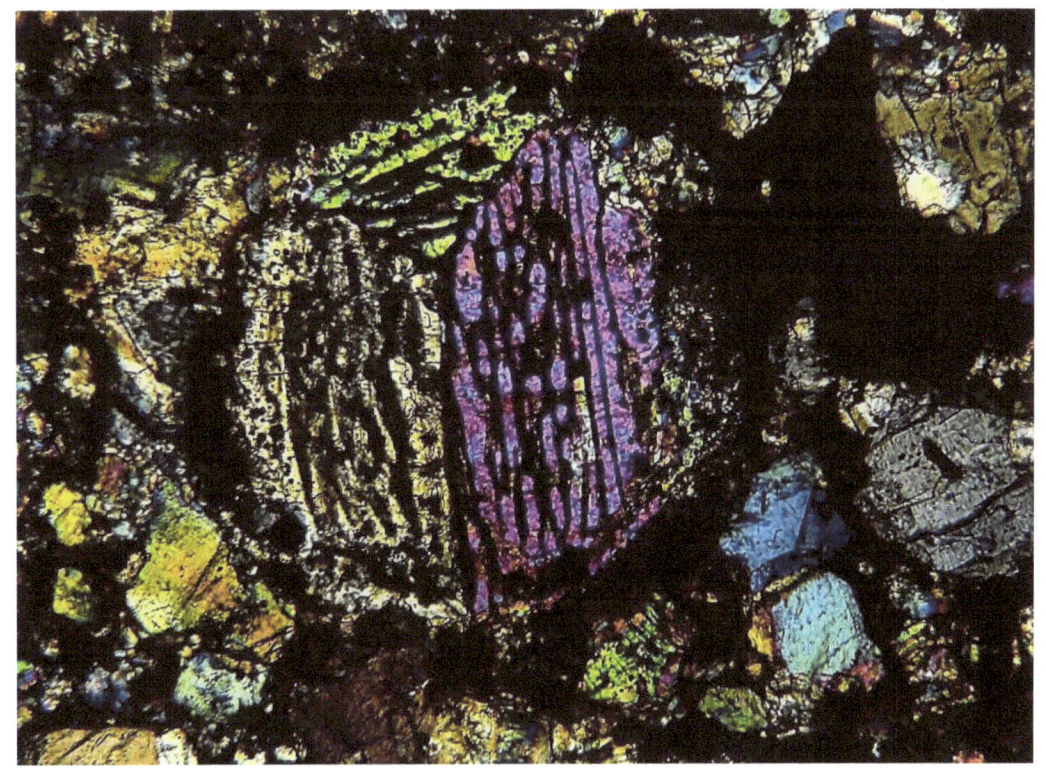

CONCEPTION JUNCTION

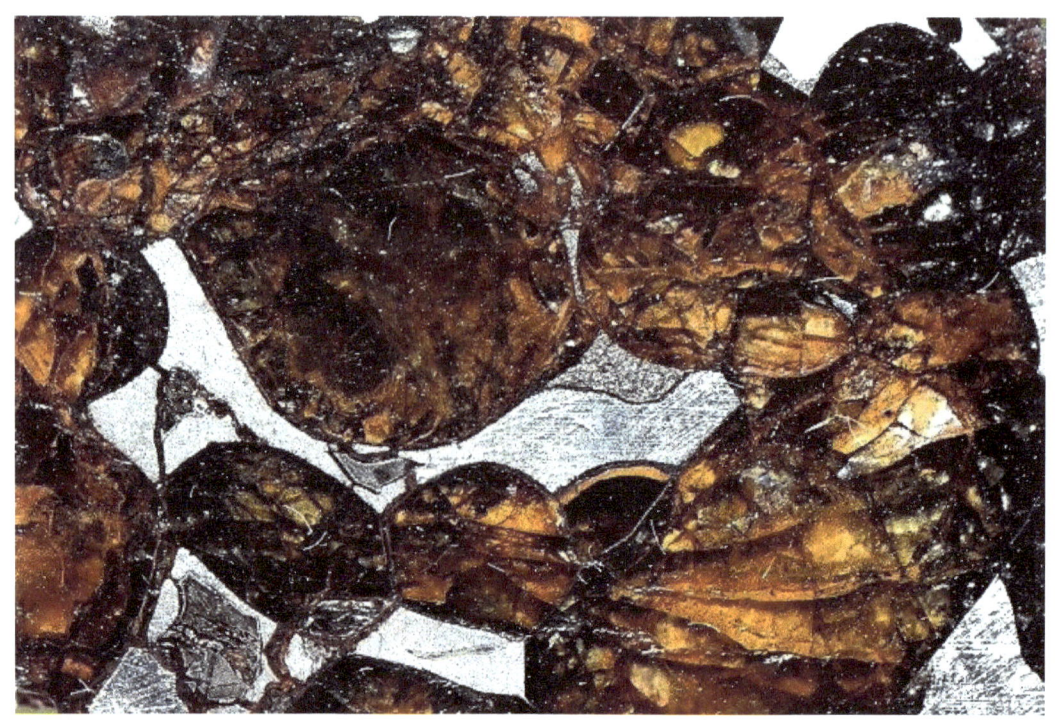

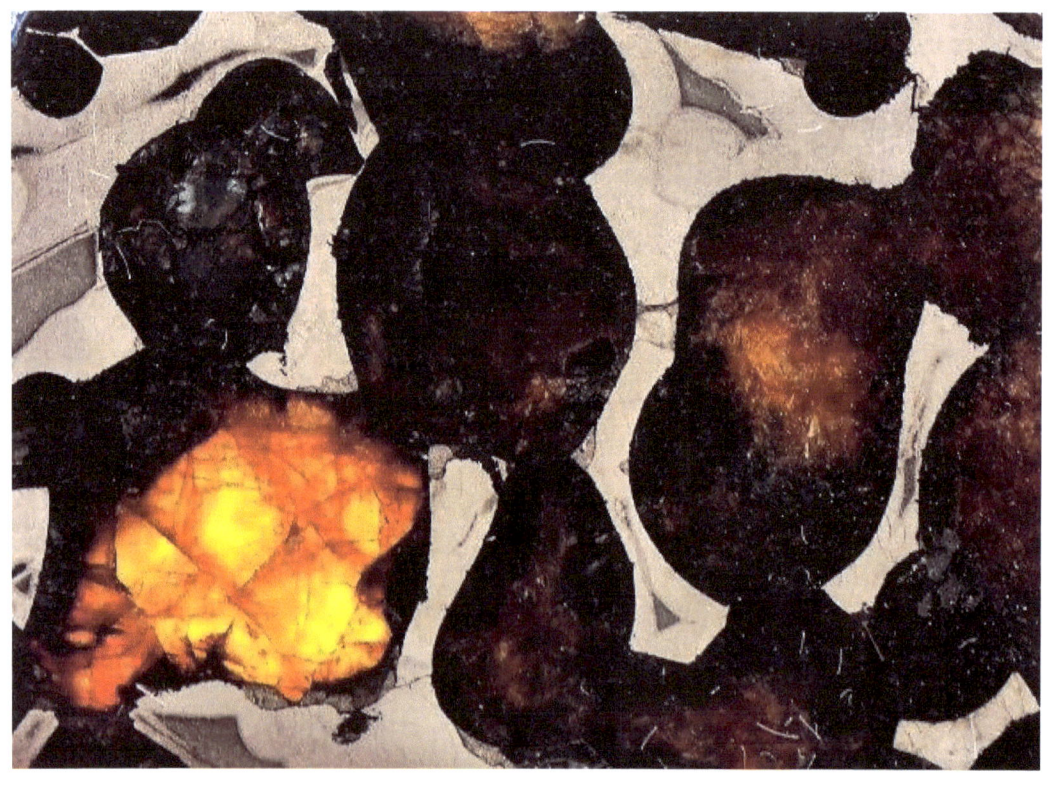

ESQUEL

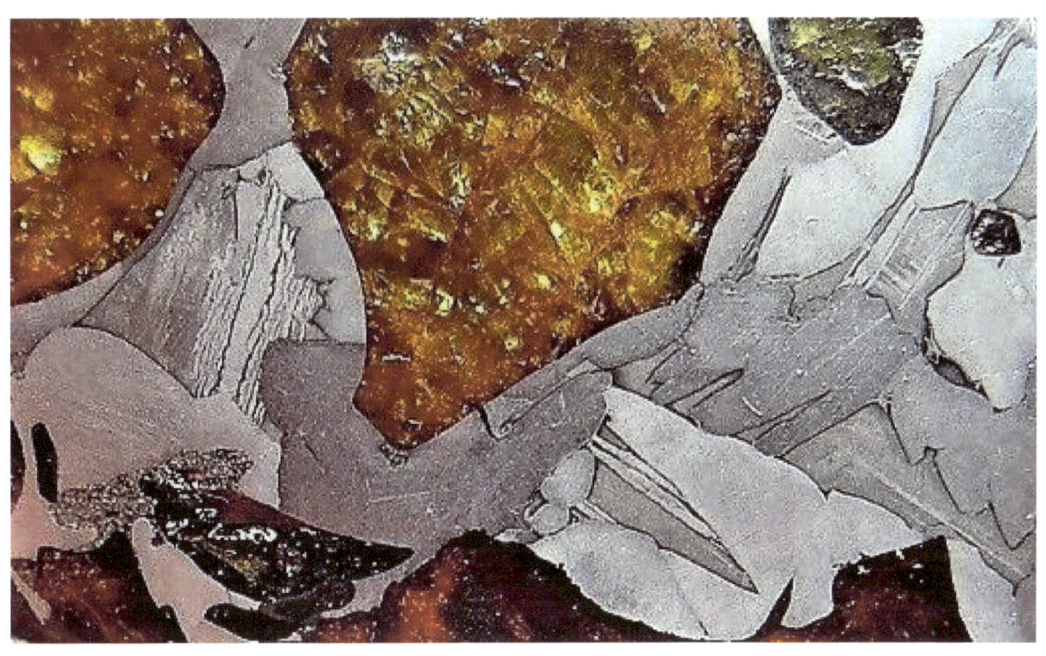

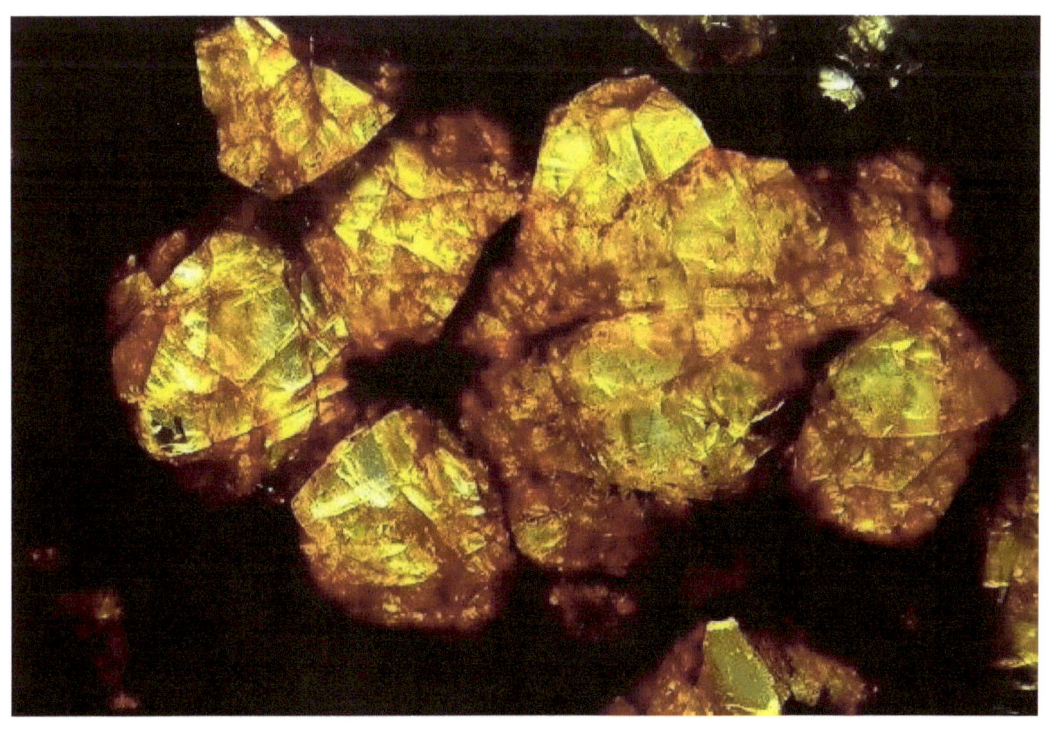

ESQUEL

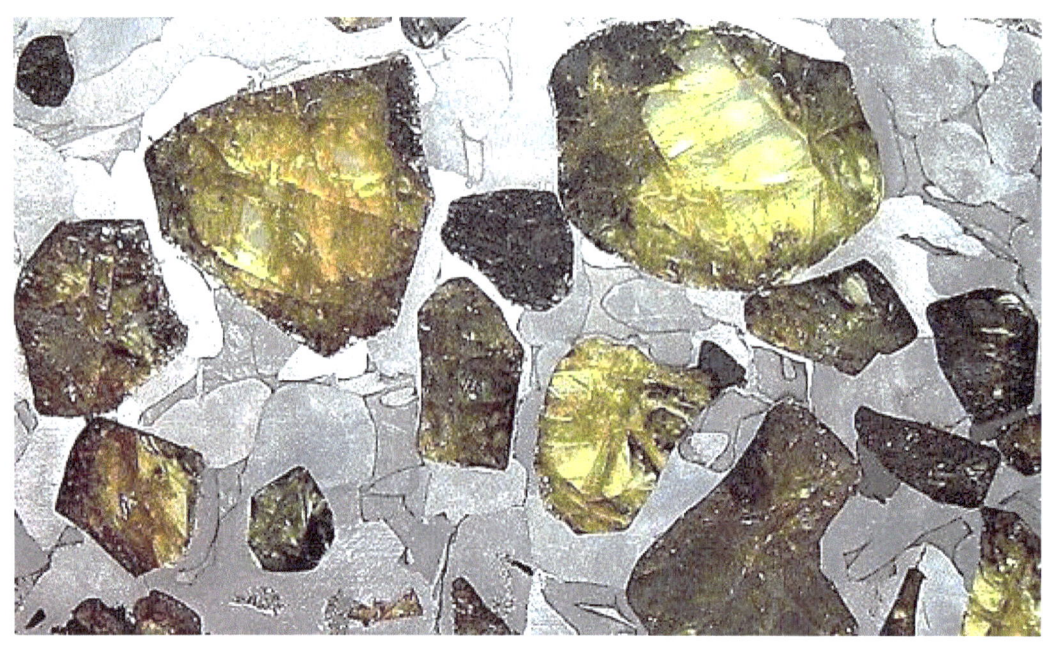

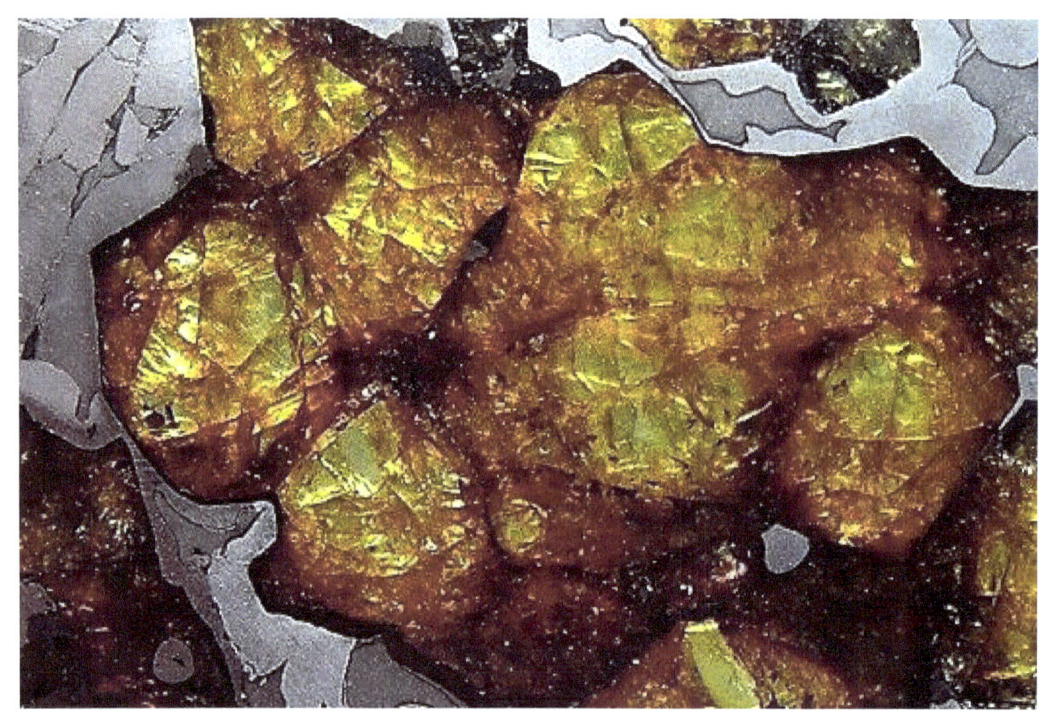

FUKANG

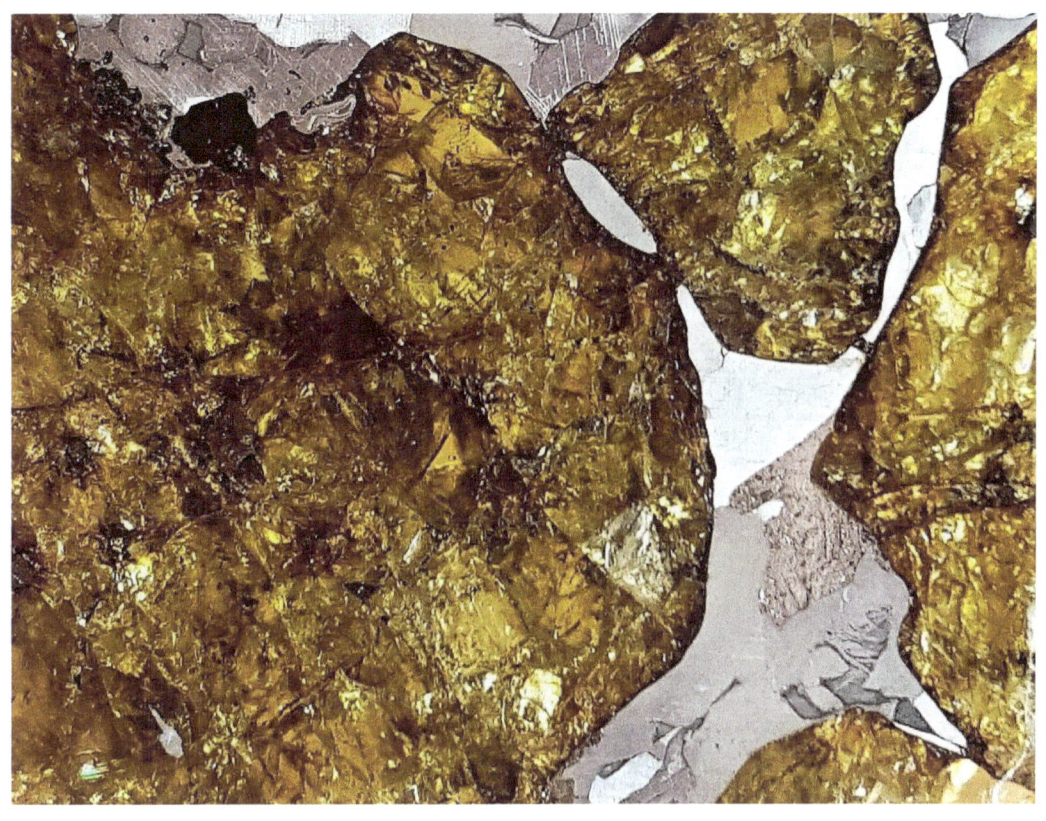

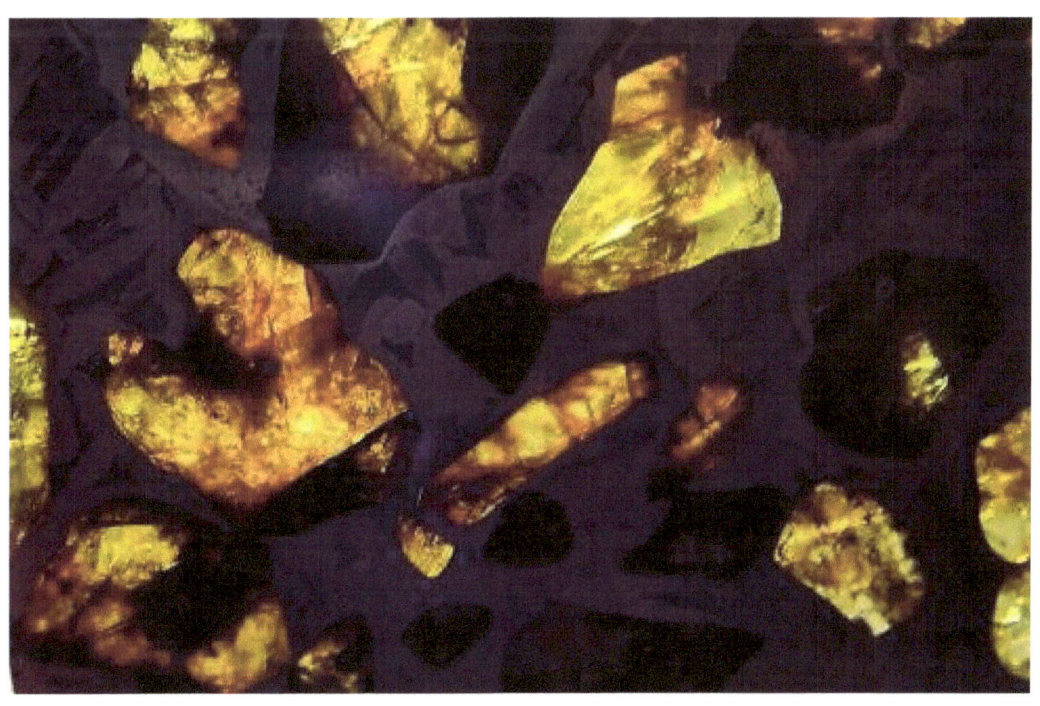

FUKANG

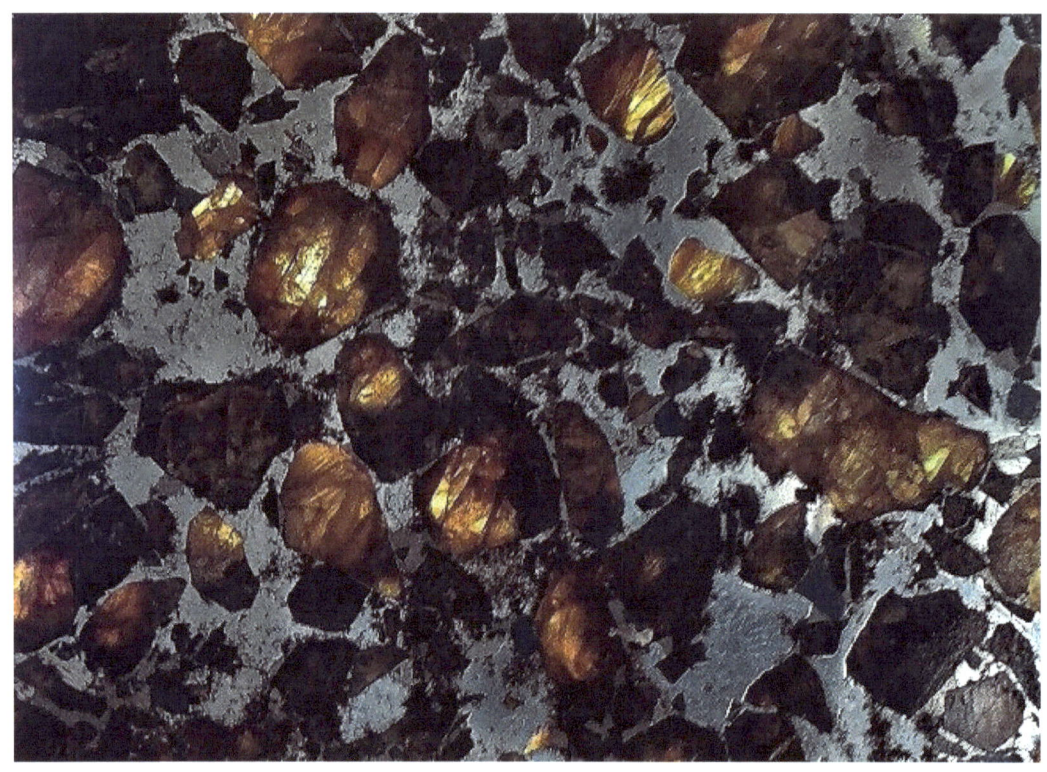

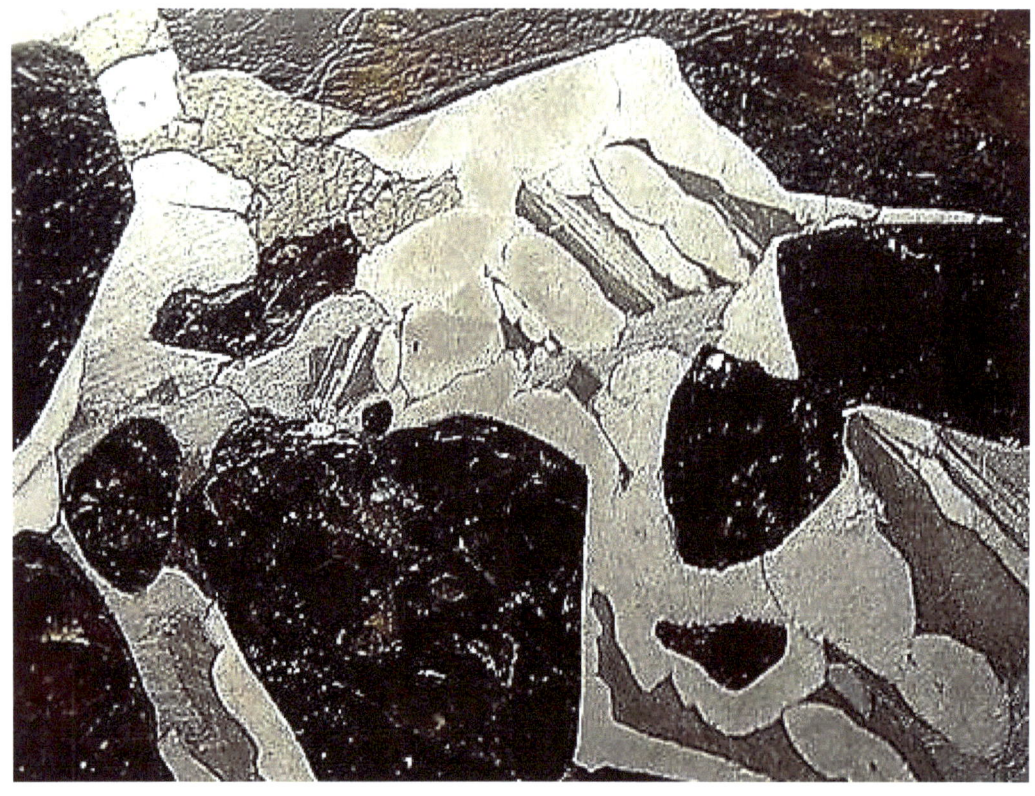